GEORG SIMMEL AND THE AMERICAN PROSPECT

GEORG SIMMEL AND THE AMERICAN PROSPECT

Gary D. Jaworski

STATE UNIVERSITY OF NEW YORK PRESS

Published by
State University of New York Press, Albany

For information, address State University of New York
Press, State University Plaza, Albany, N.Y. 12246

Production by E. Moore
Marketing by Bernadette LaManna

Library of Congress Cataloging-in-Publication Data

Jaworski, Gary D., 1954-
    Georg Simmel and the American prospect / Gary D. Jaworski.
        p.   cm.
    Includes bibliographical references and index.
    ISBN 0-7914-3172-X (pb : alk. paper). — ISBN 0-7914-3171-1 (hc :
alk. paper)
    1. Simmel, Georg, 1858-1918. 2. Sociology—United States.
I. Title.
HM22.U5J39 1997
301'.092—dc20
                                                                    96-3552
                                                                    CIP

10 9 8 7 6 5 4 3 2 1

To the memory of my father,
Walter Michael Jaworski

CONTENTS

CONTENTS

PREFACE

These essays are the result of an extended meditation on the American reception of Georg Simmel, the German philosopher and sociologist. This prolonged engagement with matters Simmelian began when I was an undergraduate student. Peter Freund, one of my professors who was then exploring the sociology of health and illness (Freund 1982), introduced me to Simmel's essay on the "Sociology of the Senses," translated in Park and Burgess's "green bible," *Introduction to the Science of Sociology* (Park and Burgess 1969 [1921]). The essay was suggestive, hardly adequate, but it piqued my interest in Simmel, an interest that I cultivated during graduate studies at the New School for Social Research in New York City. There studying Simmel became an opportunity and an escape.

The New School tradition of teaching the works of Georg Simmel extends as far back as Albert Salomon, an original member of the Graduate Faculty of Political and Social Sciences, whose writings and seminars on Simmel are discussed here for the first time. The tradition continued in the work of Alfred Schutz, who "paid homage" (Wagner 1970: 49) to Simmel in some of his wartime papers on applied social theory (e.g., Schutz 1971 [1944]), and then later in the courses of Peter Berger, Stanford M. Lyman, and Guy Oakes, among others. But during my course work in the late 1970s and early 1980s, it was not Simmel but Weber, and Marx especially, who dominated the intellectual discussions of professor and student alike. These intellectual discussions were animated and exciting, but also contentious and interminable. Finding it difficult to distinguish myself within the crowd of contending Weberian and Marxian scholars, I specialized instead in the study of Simmel. This decision provided a way of both defining my own intellectual interests and linking with the New School tradition. Given my circumstances at the time, this strategy proved more successful than leaving the New

School to pursue a degree elsewhere, as some of my fellow students
were doing.

The decision to direct my attention to Simmel was made in
my first year of graduate studies, while I was a Teacher's Assistant to
Benjamin Nelson, the noted Weber scholar and author of *The Idea of
Usury* (Nelson 1969). It was also aided by a fortuitous discovery.
Nelson had served as a series editor for Harper Torchbooks, and
copies of the books in one of his series, "Researches in the Social,
Cultural and Behavioral Sciences," could be found in his New School
office. Among the many books was Kurt H. Wolff's Commemorative
Volume on Simmel (1965), a companion to the one on Durkheim
(1960). Both volumes were originally published in the late 1950s by
the Ohio State University Press, but in the mid-1960s they were
republished by Harper & Row in Nelson's series. I "borrowed" Nelson's copy of the Simmel volume, read it cover to cover, craved
more, and began reading everything I could find about the German
philosopher and sociologist. Nelson died in 1978, before I could
return the borrowed book, which now sits on my bookshelf awaiting
its next inquisitive borrower.

Among the literature I read was the important piece by Donald
N. Levine, Ellwood S. Carter, and Eleanor Miller Gorman, "Simmel's Influence on American Sociology," which had recently been
published (Levine et. al. 1976). This essay, a key reference for all
students of Simmel's American reception, combines broad historical
scope and detailed factual information, grand statements and suggestive aperçus. For two decades now it has provided the best portrait
of Simmel in America. And yet, it was as apparent to me then as
now that the essay manifests the faults of its qualities. Its expansive
treatment of the subject, for example, while masterfully organized,
results in a superficial handling of many issues, a limitation that is
all too apparent and disappointing. The chapters that follow seek to
correct this deficit by examining in close detail selected facets of
the American Simmel reception characteristically glossed or ignored
in the account of Levine and his colleagues.

Beyond differences in scope, there are other characteristics distinguishing their essay from the ones that follow. Among these is the
absence here of claims of Simmel's "influence" on American sociology. I have serious reservations about charting intellectual influence, partly because of opposition to that word's astrological origins, but mainly because such an approach neglects to consider the
interpretive dialectic between Simmel's writings and their readers.
Indeed, focusing on the interpretive creativity of Simmel's readers, as
opposed to the sheer force of his ideas, is consistent with the German

sociologist's own sentiments, such as when he noted: "My legacy will be, as it were in cash, distributed to many heirs, each transforming his part into use conforming to *his* nature" (Simmel quoted in Coser 1965: 24). The essays that follow, then, focus less on Simmel's ideas per se, than they do on the practical meaning or significance of his ideas for a range of American social thinkers. Consistent with this emphasis, my work gives far greater attention to archival data, biographical and contextual analysis, and where appropriate and possible interview material. I am convinced that without these kinds of data the American Simmel reception cannot fully be understood.

A final contrast can be seen in the different stories our respective studies tell. After reviewing an often erratic and disjointed Simmel reception, Levine and his colleagues conclude by drawing on the trope of progress. They tell a story of sociologists struggling to create their discipline, make it viable, and furnish it with solid, scientific foundations, and in the process drawing on different aspects of Simmel's thought. In this view, the story of Simmel in America is the story of sociology's scientific advance. Whether sociology has become, or can become, a science is a debatable issue (see Turner and Turner 1992). What is certain, however, is that the story of Simmel in America is not exhausted by an analysis of the classical sociologist's relationship to intellectual progress. In these pages I explore a new narrative: a story not of the advance of sociology but of the struggle to define America. This book reexamines the American Simmel reception in light of the conception of sociology as a conversation on America rather than a conversation sociologists have with themselves.

As Ross (1991) has shown, the social sciences have continually maintained a dialogue with American ideals and ideologies. The historical project of American exceptionalism is closely intertwined with the development of American social science. Rather than viewing the social sciences in isolation from American ideals and events, she places them at the very nexus of national developments. The present study shares Ross's historicizing impulse, the demonstration that the American social sciences constitute an ongoing dialogue with American ideals and trends. While I do not take up her investigation of American exceptionalism, I do discover in sociological thought a range of other national ideals: democracy, individuality, racial tolerance, to name a few. When examined through such an historical lense, the American Simmel reception gains a new significance. Not only a contribution to the history of sociology, as in the account of Levine and colleagues, the American Simmel reception can be read for its connections to the history of America. More specifically, that reception embodies efforts to transform American society, to shape its future, to influence the American prospect. It is these efforts, and the role of Simmel's thought in them, that constitute the central subject matter of my study.

The following chapters were written over the span of a decade. The theme of Simmel's relationship to the American prospect emerged slowly during this time and, consequently, is evident in some chapters more than others. But in all cases I told the story that was consistent with the evidence. Some early chapters, such as the one on Lewis A. Coser, reveal the theme more than some later ones, such as the Goffman chapter. Here it was the availability of supporting data—correspondence, interview, and other primary material—that determined how far I could advance the thesis. I would therefore be content to have readers evaluate the soundness of my interpretation of Simmel's reception by considering not each chapter alone but the larger project as a whole. Together, the chapters reveal a side of the American Simmel reception that was previously neglected.

In Chapter 1, I examine the early reception of Simmel's writings by the Chicago sociologists Albion W. Small, Robert E. Park, and Everett C. Hughes. This chapter examines, on the one hand, the practical or moral interests behind the intellectual programs of these men, and, on the other, the manner in which those interests shaped the reading and reception of Simmel's writings. Small encountered in Chicago a city whose industrial growth and human misery were running at full throttle. Through his lectures, through his essays and books, and through his translations of Simmel's writings into English he sought to reverse the direction of this change. If Simmel helped provide the intellectual support for Small's battle with laissez-faire policy and its alternative socialist programs, he provided Park with fertile resources to battle against biological racism. Simmel's writings not only provided purely sociological answers to the troubles of cities with diverse populations; his writings supported the liberal goals of racial tolerance and reciprocity. For Hughes, senior Simmel scholar of the postwar period, Simmel's essay on sociability provided a vision of redemption through communication, a fitting image for America in the Cold War years.

Chapter 2 examines Goffman's writings on etiquette and front and finds in them traces of a Chicago school tradition of writings on such topics. Shaped by both Spencer and Simmel, Robert E. Park launched a tradition that was followed in the writings of his students, Bertram W. Doyle and Everett C. Hughes. Goffman shared much with these authors, especially Hughes, with whom he shared the view of fronts as manipulative shields of self-interest. Misunderstandings of Spencer's thought by Park and Doyle were adopted by Goffman, who accepted the functionalist assumption of the necessity of fronts. This assumption limits the liberative potential of Goffman's thought, a limitation not found in Simmel's writings. During the 1960s, Goffman rejected the antinomialism of the youthful rebels, insisting that selves can be manipulated and played with, but not abandoned. In Simmelian terms, Goffman sought an accommodation of form and life. In doing so, he mirrored Park's conservatism more than Simmel's liberalism.

The fate of Simmel's writings in the intellectual system of Talcott Parsons is the subject of chapter 3. Here I provide an analysis of the drafted section on Simmel for *The Structure of Social Action*, among other unpublished manuscripts, and I explain why Parsons chose to omit that section from the published book. My account of this curious ommission follows Buxton (1985) and others in emphasizing the moral pathos and other practical concerns underlying Parsons's early writings. Parsons's efforts to shore up moral consensus in the post-Depression years, and his intellectual competition with Howard P. Becker, I argue, fatefully shaped Parsons's early Simmel reception.

In chapter 4, "A Note on Kaspar D. Naegele," I discuss one of Parsons's students, a family friend of the Simmels' in Germany, and a student of Simmel's thought. Naegele was interested in Simmel's dualisms and paradoxical formulations, his tendency to look at social forms first from one category and then from the opposite. There may have been an elective affinity between Simmel's views on the tragedy of culture and Naegele's generation, which had witnessed the human tragedy wrought by Nazism and world war. But the concept of tragedy did not easily fit into Parsonian functionalism, and Naegele's efforts to link Simmel and Parsons were frustrated.

In the mid-1950s, Robert K. Merton undertook a close reading of Simmel's *Soziologie*. Chapter 5 explores the results of that effort in relation to both Merton's development of his own brand of functionalist analysis and his confrontation with the problematic relation between democracy and bureaucracy in postwar America. From Simmel's writings on "visibility" Merton drew lessons for democratic leadership in modern, bureaucratic societies.

Lewis A. Coser's attempt to find a language for his critical impulses led him to Merton's functionalism and to a Mertonian interpretation of Simmel's ideas on conflict. Chapter 6 explores Coser's reception of Simmel in relation to these biographical and

intellectual developments, on the one hand, and in relation to
Coser's attempt to advance the cause of workers in industrial America, on the other. The "positive functions of conflict" sanctioned
the cause of worker struggles and strikes, as well as of the nonviolent
resistance of the nascent civil rights movement.

Albert Salomon was invited to join the University in Exile,
later renamed the New School for Social Research, in order to represent the Weberian approach to sociology. Indeed, it is from his
writings on Weber and on French social thought that he his best
known. But Salomon was also a student of Simmel's at Berlin and he
gained a unique perspective on the classical sociologist, which he
brought to his students and other audiences in his unpublished writings and seminars on Simmel. Chapter 7 presents Salomon's most
sustained discussion of Simmel's work. In an introduction and set of
explanatory notes, I describe the provenance and significance of this
important essay. The justification for including it in this book goes
beyond my own role in bringing the piece to publication. Salomon's
little-known essay deserves wider recognition. It is my hope that
including it in this volume will contribute to increased attention
to Salomon's role in the American Simmel reception.

Finally chapter 8 examines current efforts to situate Simmel
within the intellectual movement of postmodernism. What social
concerns does this movement manifest? What contributions to social
change does it seek to make? Answers to questions such as these by
Deena Weinstein and Michael A. Weinstein, among others, bring
this story of Simmel's reception in America to its conclusion.

ACKNOWLEDGMENTS

What wisdom exists in these pages was forged in the intellectual atmosphere and tradition of the New School for Social Research.
Of this tradition, I have learned the most from Arthur J. Vidich,
Stanford M. Lyman, and Guy Oakes; as well as my other teachers,
especially Benjamin N. Nelson, Joseph Bensman, and Robert Lilien-
feld.

Most of my professors expressed little sympathy for sociological
functionalism. Three representatives of this approach—Talcott Parsons, Robert K. Merton, and Lewis A. Coser—however, were warmly
receptive and helpful to me. A year before his death, Talcott Parsons responded with interest and encouragement to my query about
his manuscript on Simmel. His letter convinced Victor Lidz, Parsons's literary executor, to send me a copy of the unpublished
manuscript on Simmel discussed in chapter 3. I feel privileged to
have been one of the first persons to have read this manuscript after
it was "discovered." I feel privileged, also, to have had the opportunity to exchange correspondence on matters Parsonian with Victor
Lidz. Robert K. Merton granted me two interviews and access to relevant unpublished writings. Lewis A. Coser also granted two interviews and read and commented on a draft of chapter 6. There is no
doubt that they would not agree with all that has been written about
them; nevertheless, this study has benefited from their support and
encouragement.

Others who have assisted with information or commentary on
earlier versions of these chapters include William Buxton, Elaine
and John Cumming, Rick Helmes-Hayes, David Frisby, Donald N.
Levine, Shan Nelson-Rowe, Alan Sica, Greg Smith, Andrew Travers,
Douglas G. Webb, Yves Winkin, Kurt H. Wolff, and Philipp O.
Naegele, who gave permission and assisted with my study of his
brother's correspondence and papers. Material from the Talcott Par-

sons Papers is quoted with permission of the Harvard University Archives. Material from the Robert E. Park Papers and Everett C. Hughes Papers is quoted with permission of the University of Chicago Library. The professionalism and courtesy of Clark Elliott at the Harvard University Archives, and of Richard L. Popp at the University of Chicago Library, are gratefully acknowledged. Fairleigh Dickinson University provided regular released time without which most of these essays would not have been written. The research for chapter 1 was supported by National Endowment for the Humanities grant #FT-38554-93.

I should like to thank the following people for assisting with my research of Salomon's papers and for making possible the publication of his essay: Arthur J. Vidich (New York), Thomas Luckmann (Frankfurt), Ilja Srubar (Nurnberg), Diane R. Spielmann (New York) of the Leo Baeck Institute, and Hubert Knoblauch (Constance), current director of the Sozialwissenschaftliches Archiv, Universität Konstanz, who has granted permission to publish the essay. The original manuscript is located in the Albert Salomon Papers (file number 28.1) of the Archive at Constance. My thanks also to Guy Oakes, Gerd Schroeter, and Patrick Watier, all of whom made suggestions for improving the manuscript; and to Jackie Bell, who provided needed secretarial assistance. A final word of gratitude goes to my wife, Laurie Erickson.

The following chapters have been revised from previously published essays, and are reprinted here with permission. Chapter 1 was originally published in *International Journal of Politics, Culture, and Society*, Vol. 8, No. 3, (Spring 1995): 389–417. Chapter 2 was published by the University of Texas Press in *Sociological Inquiry*, Vol. 66, No. 2 (1996). Chapter 3 is reprinted by permission of Kluwer Academic Publishers from *Georg Simmel and Contemporary Sociology*, edited by Michael Kaern, Bernard S. Phillips, and Robert S. Cohen, Kluwer, Boston, 1990:109–130. Chapter 5 was published in *Sociological Theory*, Vol. 8, No. 1, (1990): 99–105. Chapter 6 appeared in *Sociological Theory*, Vol. 9, No. 1 (1991): 116–123. Chapter 7 was previously published in *International Journal of Politics, Culture, and Society*, Vol. 8, No. 3 (1995): 361–378. Chapter 8 first appeared in *Simmel Newsletter*, Vol. 3, No. 2 (1993): 152–162.

PART ONE

Simmel and the Chicago Sociologists

INTRODUCTION

In this first section, there are two essays that initiate a new historiography of the American Simmel reception. In the traditional approach, analysts identify similarities between the concepts or arguments of Simmel and some American figure. The similarities between those intellectual products are then recorded and reasons for their similarity are speculatively advanced. Typically, it is argued that Simmel "influenced" the American sociologist, shaping his or her thought in profound ways.

Simmel has indeed had a profound impact on American sociological thought. But that impact is not based on the force of ideas alone. It is also a product of moral and ideological conflict, of similarity in ethical vision, of the strategic value of Simmel's ideas for contending intellectual groups. Uncovering these components of the American Simmel reception requires going beyond the traditional approach discussed above. It involves an analysis of the extratheoretical aspects of intellectual reception. This includes situating Simmel's American audience not only within intellectual space, but within the moral or ethical space of the time. It also includes going beyond what a text says to what it means. Because sociological texts are bound up with the context within which they are produced, their meaning must be understood, at least in part, in terms of that context. This is accomplished by reading those texts as historical products of strategic social action. What cultural battles are being waged, by whom, and for what ends? Reading Simmel's American reception from within the terrain of social conflict over ideas and ideals uncovers otherwise hidden aspects of that reception.

In Chapter 1, "Translation as Social Action: The Early American Simmel Translations," I interpret the Simmel translations by Albion Small, Robert E. Park, and Everett C. Hughes from this new point of view. While it is perfectly necessary and legitimate to evaluate translations for their degree of accuracy, I chose to view them for their strategic value. The selection of texts to translate, the timing of their publication, the translation of words and ideas, the interpretation of meaning—all, I contend, may be considered forms of strategic social action. The chapter presents a reading of the Chicago School translations of Simmel from within the perspective of the translators' political battles: of Small's battle with advocates of laissez-faire and socialism, of Park's rejection of biological racism, of Hughes's struggles with war and intolerance. While the Chicago figures had good intellectual reasons for an interest in Simmel's writings, my analysis shows the extratheoretical components of that interest. Simmel was good to translate because he served these larger social purposes.

Erving Goffman was a product of the Chicago sociology department even as he transcended its framework. While his indebtedness to Everett Hughes is obvious, his deeper connections to the Chicago intellectual and ethical traditions are often neglected. In chapter 2, those connections are revealed by discussing Goffman's involvement in a neglected intellectual tradition. Goffman adhered to the view of his teachers that social masks were a necessary element of social life; they were to be played with or hidden behind, but not discarded. As such, Goffman sided against the romantic yearnings of the sixties youth movement, which expressed the desire to shed all social masks in favor of natural expression. Expressed in Simmelian language, Goffman proposed an accommodation between life and form, an intellectual and ethical development that limits the liberative potential of his work.

CHAPTER 1

TRANSLATION AS SOCIAL ACTION: THE EARLY AMERICAN SIMMEL TRANSLATIONS

The history of sociology is in need of a new historical narrative, a story that reflects and reinforces the contemporary transition in sociological thought from a celebration of scientific autonomy to a demonstration of social relevance. Whether they are accomplished through critical analysis of sociological discourse (Stehr 1986), historical analysis of sociology's changing publics (Buxton and Turner 1992), or pragmatic proposals for change (Seidman 1992), sociology's aspirations to professional and intellectual self-sufficiency have been pronounced a failure. Not only has the discipline failed to achieve scientific status, it has, with few exceptions, alienated itself from key audiences by withdrawing from participation in civic discourse. The new narrative that I envision responds to recent calls to renew the social contract of sociology with its broader publics (Halliday and Janowitz 1992). It will take the form of studies which feature the historical and contemporary contributions of sociology to moral-political issues. These studies will tell a story not of the advance of sociology but of the struggle to define America.

This chapter reexamines the American Simmel reception in light of the conception of sociology as a conversation on America rather than a conversation sociologists have with themselves.[1] It views sociologists as creative figures, like poets and novelists, who help to shape America's future by molding how we think about it. While sociologists typically exercise little formal power in society, they can wield considerable influence informally through their writings as well as through their classroom lectures, curriculum decisions, and organizational activities. Through their roles as scholars and citizens, sociologists participate in defining the direction of this country to successive generations of Americans.

Mannheim (1982) drew attention to this "supra-theoretical capacity" of thought to both apprehend and transform social reality when he argued that "all sociological thought is originally embedded in a drive for change" (Mannheim 1982: 199). What Marx in the *Theses on Feuerbach* considered a political desideratum, Mannheim conceived as a premise of sociological analysis. Research that is guided by this assumption, Mannheim proposed, must examine both the contextual background and transformative purposes of social thought. This approach directs analysis away from the systematics of thought, focusing on thinkers' conceptual contributions to cumulative theory, and toward the history of theory-in-use, analyzing the role of ideas in local experiential contexts (cf. Merton 1967).

When examined in this light, the American Simmel reception gains a new significance. Not only a contribution to the history of sociology, the American Simmel reception can be read for its connections to the history of America. More specifically, that reception embodies efforts to transform American society, to shape its future, to influence the American prospect. It is these efforts, and the role of Simmel's thought in them, that constitute the central subject matter of my study. The writings and translations of Simmel by Albion W. Small, Robert E. Park, and Everett C. Hughes provide an instructive example of what is at stake in such an analysis. While an understanding of Simmel's reception by these three Chicago sociologists cannot be reduced to an analysis of their practical interests and strategic aims, such an analysis adds a new dimension to the story of Simmel in America.

THE RIOT OF IMAGINATION AND THE ORDER OF INVESTIGATION

The last quarter of the nineteenth century was a period of great intellectual insecurity. As urbanization, industrialization, and immigration changed the pace and shape of American life, disparate voices of contending classes struggled for public attention and political influence. Friends of Humanity and Friends of Capital offered differing views on the central issues of the day: the former demanding change, the latter wanting society left alone. If both sought to influence public sympathies and sensibilities, neither attained unrivaled legitimacy.

This ideological confusion, coupled with an inchoate and anachronistic system of graduate education in the United States

(Storr 1953), led unprecedented numbers of young intellectuals to travel abroad in order to attain some mental and moral purchase on problems at home. They traveled mostly to Germany, and in the 1870s–1880s to the universities of Berlin and Leipzig, the two centers of German scholarship at the time (Herbst 1965: 16–18). Leipzig, the home of Wundt's famed psychology laboratory, had long been a popular destination of Americans studying abroad. And Berlin, the capital of the new German Empire, was home base for a galaxy of leading German academics, including Gierke, Ranke, Mommsen, Dilthey, Helmholtz, Schmoller, and Paulsen. Albion Woodbury Small was a member of the generation of American intellectuals who came to Germany in the 1870s and 1880s. He studied at Berlin in 1879–1880 and at Leipzig and the British Museum a year later. While Small was at Berlin studying with Gustav Schmoller (Herbst 1965), the German political economist, Georg Simmel was there studying philosophy. Dr. Small and Dr. Simmel would later meet, perhaps through Schmoller, a mutual friend. Their intellectual relationship contributes a central chapter to the American Simmel reception.

Small returned to America with both an admiration for German *Wissenschaft*, the scholarly study of specialized subjects, and an esteem for German scholars as framers of social policy. German scholars were organized and active in formulating national policy. Small was especially impressed with the scholars associated with the *Verein für Sozialpolitik*—who included his professor Gustav Schmoller—men who battled advocates of laissez-faire and socialism alike (Bernert 1982). In contrast, Small's America was morally and politically rent and lacked a group with cultural authority capable of mending the social fabric. Following the German model, Small sought to carve out a region of cultural authority and consensus within the chaotic world of urban America. His vision was expressed in the conclusion to the volume on *General Sociology*: if society is to be properly guided, "there must be credible sociologists in order that there may be farseeing economists and statesmen and moralists" (Small 1905a: 729).

Small made modest attempts to institutionalize his vision, first as professor (1881–1889), then as President (1889–1892) of Colby College in his home state of Maine. When in 1892 he was called by William Rainey Harper to head the first Department of Sociology, however, his vision was given a vital foundation. The place would be the University of Chicago; the discipline would be sociology; the means would be the graduate program, the scientific journal, and the professional society.

In these efforts, Small was certainly guided by his religious roots in the social gospel (Greek 1992; Ahlstrom 1975: 264–65). Small's Baptist education and faith, as Dibble (1975: 147) has shown, are closely interwoven with his politics and sociology. His belief in the brotherhood of man and the benefits of a Christian cooperative commonwealth formed the basis of his relentless opposition to the pervasive dogma of laissez-faire. And a commitment to religious gradualism may have been behind his opposition to the many late nineteenth-century socialist programs, with their apocalyptic and millennialist tone. But Small was guided as well by what Hollinger (1991) has called the "intellectual gospel." With this term Hollinger refers to the convictions, practices, and discourse of those intellectuals of the late nineteenth century who, while remaining committed to Christianity, felt enthusiasm for the ethic of science. The intellectual gospel is "the belief that conduct in accord with the ethic of science could be religiously fulfilling, a form of 'justification'" (Hollinger 1991: 123). While the social gospel motivated social reform, sanctifying work in settlement houses or the Progressive political movement, the intellectual gospel stimulated the academic reform that resulted in the rise of the large research university, sanctifying work in the lab or archive (Hollinger 1991: 134). Supplementing and in some cases replacing prayer with knowledge and worship with research, these intellectuals, Louis Agassiz, T. H. Huxley, and Woodrow Wilson among them, chose science as a religious calling.

Hollinger (1991: 126) characterizes Johns Hopkins University, the model for American research universities in the late nineteenth and early twentieth centuries, and the institution where in 1889 Small took his Ph.D., as "the most ideologically intense bastion of the intellectual gospel in the United States." Daniel Coit Gilman, president of Johns Hopkins, was an admirer of the German system of education in general, and of the University of Berlin in particular, and incorporated into his innovative educational reforms a number of German practices and ideals: the Ph.D. degree, the seminar, the principles of *lehrfreiheit* and *lernfreiheit*, and the scientific journal (Hawkins 1960: 16; Franklin 1910: 227–28). Small took these elements of the "religion of research" (Herbst 1965, p. 31) with him and proselytized for the secularized faith as chair of the Department of Sociology at the University of Chicago. There he formulated the first commandment of graduate schools in the religious idiom: "Remember the research ideal, to keep it holy" (Small, 1905b: 87).

The social gospel and the intellectual gospel together guided Small's interest in and reception of the works of Georg Simmel. If the social gospel defined Small's ends, the creation of a Christian cooperative commonwealth, it also defined his adversaries, proponents of the anti-Christian laissez-faire doctrine. The intellectual gospel provided the means for achieving those ends, professional training in social research.

These considerations add a new dimension to our understanding of the intellectual kinship between Small and Simmel. As others have shown (Levine, Carter, and Gorman 1976: 815–17), both men were attempting to define sociology as an independent discipline. But if for Simmel the "problem of sociology" was primarily a theoretical and philosophical question, for Small it was also a question of profound practical significance. It would grant to sociologists alone the cultural authority then distributed among the many contenders for social influence. Pastors, politicians, and the public would then be obliged to turn to sociology for answers to contemporary problems. By the turn of the century, Small was convinced that sociology had approached such a level of indispensability, calling "unpardonable" the efforts of "any man to offer himself as guide in our maze of human difficulty, unless he has got such help from available sociology that he can bring to bear upon the problems he confronts" (Small 1899: 391).

Small's efforts to transform sociology into a cognitively privileged discourse were institutionalized in the *American Journal of Sociology* (*AJS*), edited by Small from its inception in 1895 to his death in 1926. The first issue of the journal grandly announced that the "era of sociology" had begun (Small 1895a). Sociology was portrayed as a response to the times: to the extensive economic interdependence, the acute bewilderment with one's fellow citizens, and the plethora of programs for social change. The new discipline was needed to counteract attempts of the educated and uneducated alike to turn their "meager knowledge into social doctrine and policy" (p. 3). In place of these popular philosophies produced by "the riot of imagination," professional sociologists would substitute "the order of investigation" (p. 7). *AJS* would provide a voice for academic sociological doctrines: professional yet accessible, practical yet visionary. It would provide "a factor of restraint upon premature sociological opinion, a means of promoting the development of a just and adequate social philosophy, and an element of strength and support in every wise endeavor to insure the good of men" (p. 15).

SIMMEL BETWEEN CONSERVATISM AND RADICALISM

The *AJS* was not the first American scholarly journal to introduce Simmel to an American audience. In fact, it was a relative latecomer to this task. The Cornell University philosophy journal, *The Philosophical Review*, published extensive and favorable reviews of Simmel's books beginning with its first volume in 1892. In addition, the *International Journal of Ethics* in 1893, and *Annals of the American Academy of Political and Social Science* in 1895, both published translations of Simmel's works prior to the first *AJS* translation in 1896. As Frisby (1992: 156) notes, "This reception was due not merely to individual initiatives but also to the wave of American students studying in German universities." The reviews in *The Philosophical Review*, for example, were written by American philosophers who had studied at Berlin: Frank Thilly—whose Berlin associates included Edward Alsworth Ross (Ross, 1936: 37)—and Walter G. Everett and Charles M. Bakewell, both of whom most likely had heard Simmel's lectures. Simmel's involvement with the *Annals* was also furthered by an American abroad, Samuel McCune Lindsay, who included Berlin in his grand tour of European universities in 1891–1894. Lindsay edited the "Sociological Notes" of the early issues of the *Annals*, with the cooperation of Simmel (see *Annals*, Vol. 6: xi, 562), among others, and in 1900–1902 was president of the Academy.[2]

The early numbers of the *American Journal of Sociology* regularly cited the American and European publications of Simmel's works before they were translated in the *Journal* (e.g., Small 1895b; Vincent 1896; Tufts 1896). And the *International Monthly*, later renamed the *International Quarterly*, a New York journal with Simmel and Giddings of Columbia University on the advisory board, published two translations of Simmel's works: "Tendencies in German Life and Thought Since 1870" (1902) and "Fashion" (1904). The *AJS* was, however, the first American professional journal to systematically translate the German sociologist's works, publishing nine papers by Simmel under Small's editorship[3] (see Table 1).

These translations were the result of a deliberate plan on the part of Small and his colleagues to promote Simmel's work and the intellectual issues he pursued. As Small (1925: 84) commented retrospectively: "We fondly hoped that not only sociologists but social scientists in general in all English-speaking countries would respond [to the translations], if not to the extent of adopting Simmel's theories, at least to the extent of general admission that science without a recognized methodology is unthinkable." Focusing on Simmel and on the "fundamental problems of methodology"—that is, the philosophical and conceptual foundations of sociology—provided for more than just the advance of theoretical issues in sociology. It supported Small's efforts to advance the American prospect by combating Her-

TABLE 1 Simmel in the *AJS*: The First 15 Years

Volume and Year		Title
Vol. 2	1896–1897	"Superiority and Subordination as Subject–Matter of Sociology"
Vol. 3–4	1897–1898	"The Persistence of Social Groups"
Vol. 5	1898–1899	"A Chapter in the Philosophy of Value"
Vol. 8	1902–1903	"The Number of Members as Determining the Sociological Form of the Group"
Vol. 9	1903–1904	"The Sociology of Conflict"
Vol. 11	1905	"A Contribution to the Sociology of Religion"
Vol. 11	1906	"The Sociology of Secrecy and Secret Societies"
Vol. 15	1909	"The Problem of Sociology"
Vol. 16	1910	"How Is Society Possible?"

bert Spencer, the arch-intellectual champion of laissez faire.

As Hofstadter (1955) has shown, the "vogue of Spencer" was protracted, extensive, and insidious. Spencer's extension of Darwin's understanding of natural selection to the social order supported political ultraconservatism, ethical fatalism, and practical do-nothingism. It also provided the Friends of Capital with scientific justification for their campaign of ruthless acquisition and social indifference. By portraying the "survival of the fittest" as a natural law, Spencerian doctrine supported the repudiation all state involvement in the social order, including the rejection of humane efforts to attenuate the ravages of industrial growth. The politics of indifference continued unabated, if not unchallenged, through the 1890s. All of this was anathema for Small, who viewed "'natural selection' . . . today [as] a problem not a solution" (Small 1896a: 310). Small rejected the views of those he called "dogmatists of societary fatalism" (Small 1916: 199), those who argued that "whatever is in society is right, or if not right at least unavoidable" (Small 1896c: 581). The early issues of the *AJS* set out to discredit this Spencerian view, and Simmel's assistance was enlisted in this effort.

According to a leading philosophy of science of the late nineteenth century (Mill 1872), science proceeded by induction, the generalization from meticulously gathered evidence, rather than through deduction, the logical reasoning from first principles. This privileging of induction over deduction accompanied a repudiation of metaphysics, dogma, obiter dicta—all associated with the discredited theology of the past. It also legitimated two forms of critique: charges of provincialism and prematurity. Charges of provincialism were leveled against writers who generalize from a narrow base of knowledge to all of society. Such authors, specialists in biology or economics, for example, fashion grand and universal claims from restricted evidence. Provincialism of this sort flourished in England following the publication of Darwin's *Origins*, as Henry Adams noted in his *Education* (Adams 1961 [1918]: 224). The related charge of prematurity applied to those who lack the scientific humility to admit, with Small (1898: 393), "that we have as yet relatively little sociological knowledge which deserves to be dignified as 'science.'" According to Small, proper science must reject the hasty quest for final results and accept "the importance of correct beginnings" (Small 1896b: 315):

> Every person with an *a priori* theory or programme about society; every person who wants to divide up the facts of human experience into convenient little blocks of toy knowledge with which he may play science; every person who wants to pretend that he understands the laws of influence in society, resents the connotations of our method. It means that we know comparatively little about society yet, and that it will take a long, hard, combined labor, by many searchers and organizers working within sight of each other, to get the social facts into such shape that they will tell us much general truth. (Small 1898: 393)

In "The Methodology of the Social Problem," Small (1898) aimed both barrels at Spencer's sociology: it was both premature and partial. Spencer purported to discover social laws before all the facts were in, and before they were organized and properly interpreted. Consider, for example, Spencer's attempt to work out a general understanding of the general forms of relationships between persons. Small (1898: 390) considered this enterprise one of the strongest features of Spencer's sociology, but it was undertaken without benefit of Simmel's related and pathbreaking efforts to identify and analyze the most important 'social forms,' efforts which were first being published in Small's *Journal*. Any generalizations based on Spencer's incomplete data were, therefore, hasty and inadequate. While Small does not say this, such inadequate generalizations include those which supported laissez-faire.[4]

There are, of course, many motives for Small's championing of Simmel's works, including altruistic service to the intellectual community. But it seems to me that one important element in Simmel's appeal was his strategic usefulness to Small's campaign against Spencer. It should be noted that Small did not translate or promote Simmel's early sociological writings, such as *On Social Differentiation* (1890), which take up Spencerian perspectives on evolutionism and the principle of differentiation. Indeed, Simmel himself turned away from his Spencerian heritage in his later writings. Rather, Small's translations were mostly of Simmel's exercises in formal sociology, and it was these essays that would be adapted by Small for polemical purposes. These writings not only provided a reminder of what must still be accomplished in the field of sociology—the production of "an adequate schedule of the 'forms' of social life" (Small 1898, p. 391); they also provided ammunition for a critique of those efforts, like Spencer's, to propose laws based on meager foundations. According to Small, premature generalizations and provincial inductions, such as Spencer's, may attain greater value only when viewed in light of Simmel's pioneering work in formal sociology. To quote Small (1898: 391): Simmel's studies on social forms "may give value to Spencer's material . . . which it does not at present possess."

If Simmel's writings served as ammunition for the *Journal*'s criticism of conservatism, they also aided its criticism of radicalism. This side of the Simmel reception can be found in Simmel's formal introduction to the *Journal*'s readers in Volume 2: a translation of "Superiority and Subordination as Subject-Matter of Sociology" and an extensive and favorable treatment of his ideas in "The Present Status of Sociology in Germany," an essay by one of Simmel's students, Osias Thon (1897) of Berlin. The latter essay discusses the works of Simmel, Toennies, Marx, Stammler, Schmoller, and Schaeffle, among others; but Simmel is very much the hero of the piece and Marx very much the villain.

Thon introduces the problem of the scientific legitimacy of sociology, and credits Simmel with defining sociology as an independent science, thereby removing it from confusion with social philosophy, as in Toennies, or with metaphysics, as in Comte and Spencer. At the same time, Thon, like Small (1909), takes issue with Simmel for limiting the domain of sociology to the study of the forms of association alone, as opposed to their motivational contents. In Thon's view, it is neither desirable nor feasible to "treat forms of association in complete abstraction from their content" (Thon 1897: 571). "As a matter of fact," he continues, "Simmel himself, in his own sociological investigations, by no means conceives the problem in a purely formal way. On the contrary his strength is in profound and acute psychological interpretations" (Thon 1897: 571). This characterization of Simmel as social psychologist of social life is repeated later: "Simmel's method of sociological analysis is distinguished by profound psychological analysis and by historical illumination of problems, though relatively less by the latter than by the former" (Thon 1897: 736). Sociology is properly defined, then, as "the science of the forms and the psychical motivation of human association" (Thon 1897: 570).

In addition to giving sociology its raison d'être, Simmel is credited with providing powerful ammunition against Marx and historical materialism. This ammunition comes, first, from Simmel's investigations into the philosophy of history. Following Kant's analysis of the natural sciences, Simmel analyzed the intellectual presuppositions of the historical sciences. How is historical understanding possible? How is it possible to mediate the temporal distance between past and present? In answering these questions, Thon charges, "historical materialism is of no assistance," because the materialist conception of consciousness is "soulless" (Thon 1897: 579), that is, it portrays consciousness as a historical and existential variable rather than a constant, and therefore provides no basis for comprehending mentalities of the past. "So long as the search is for an explanation of historical occurrences," Thon maintained, "it will be essential for the historian to transport himself, so to speak, into the psychical conditions of the persons or groups whom he depicts. We may add that historical materialism not only does not remove this difficulty in cognitive theory, but rather increases and complicates it." In contrast, Simmel's analysis of the psychological preconditions of historical understanding solves the problem. For, according to Thon, his analysis presumes a unity of consciousness between historians and their subjects, thereby permitting "the reproduction in the mind of the investigator of the psychical conditions fundamental to the historical occurrences" (Thon 1897: 579).

In addition to contributing a more satisfactory philosophy of historical understanding than is offered by historical materialism, Simmel provided a critique of the ethical superiority of socialism. The argument for the ethical superiority of socialism derives, in part, from its purported universality: its claim to advance the interests of humanity, as opposed to the interests of one class alone. But Simmel directly contests this claim. Thon points out that Simmel, in his *Soziologie*, declared "in opposition to all previous explanations, that the psychological ground of all struggles for equality, *the socialistic* included, is endeavor after higher status, not for actual equality" (Thon 1897: 735; emphasis added). Thus Simmel demonstrated, with his "profound psychological analysis," that the motives for movements of equality "contain a vigorous individualizing element" (Thon 1897: 735, 736).

This argument is repeated and extended in Small's translation of Simmel's "Superiority and Subordination" (Simmel 1896), an essay that substitutes for the Marxian interest in domination the Simmelian principle of reciprocity. In this essay, Simmel directly contests the views of socialism and anarchism, both of which emphasize the possibility and desirability of virtually complete equality. Simmel's review of the historical record reveals case after case of movements aiming for equality resulting instead in new arrangements of superiority and subordination. In addition, Simmel takes a visionary stance: "For as long in the future as prevision can reach," he declared, "we may contest the possibility of a social constitution without superiority and inferiority" (Simmel 1896: 400). While Simmel believed that natural human differences would continue to "press for expression in external graduations of rank," he did foresee promising cultural tendencies. Stated in the form of a proposition: sorrow, humiliation, and oppression, feelings which follow from subordination to others, are reduced in direct proportion to the advance of two conditions: first, the reduction in investments of personality in work, and, second, the increase of opportunities for shared leadership (Simmel 1896: 400-3).[5] Not revolution, then, but evolution, the slow working out of progressive cultural tendencies, would bring about the changes desired by the radicals. Thus did Simmel's first appearance in the *AJS* help to further the *Journal*'s stated mission, namely, "to work against the growing popular impression that short cuts may be found to universal prosperity, and to discountenance utopian social programmes."[6]

SIMMELIAN INTERACTIONISM CONTRA BIOLOGICAL RACISM

Near the end of his life, Small expressed disappointment with the results of his efforts to promote Simmel's writings and the issues they raised. Writing in the context of a review of Nicholas Spykman's (1966 [1925]) independent efforts to provide a hearing for Simmel's works, Small declared defeat. In contrast to his high aspirations for a wide acquaintance with Simmel's writings, Small estimated that "the Americans who have given indubitable evidence of having considered Simmel thoroughly might be counted on the fingers of one hand" (Small 1966 [1925]: 84). The situation was worse in England, specifically at the London School of Economics (LSE), he believed; there he found the pages of his *Journal*, including those containing his translations of Simmel's writings, unread and even uncut.

While Simmel's writings found a wide readership on the continent—especially in Germany, of course, but also in France, Italy, and Russia (Gassen 1959: 357-75)—Small's disillusionment was well founded. American and British interest in Simmel's writings during the early decades of this century was limited, going well beyond skimpy journal citations or uncut pages at LSE.[7] British scholars, especially, displayed little interest in Simmel. This disinterest was due in part to cultural snobbery, in part to Anglo-American distaste for abstract reasoning, and in part to growing anti-German sentiment before and after World War I (Kennedy 1980).[8] Instructive in this regard is the British publication of an abridged translation of "Sociology and the Social Sciences," an essay by Emile Durkheim and Paul Fauconnet (1904). It actually omits that section of the original essay containing a discussion of Simmel's works. But if many British and American scholars were chauvinistic in their attitude toward Simmel, he too displayed his European chauvinism toward them. This point is evidenced by Simmel's refusal to attend the 1904 St. Louis Exposition. Small was a vice president, with Harvard's Hugo Münsterberg, of the Exposition's Congress of Arts and Sciences. Despite Small's efforts to secure Simmel's attendance, including a visit to Germany in the summer of 1903 (Small 1925: 87), he did not attend. Rather, Simmel derided the Exposition, calling it a "circus of celebrities" and said he would have nothing to gain from attending the conference, since he could always meet in Berlin with his noted colleagues and contemporaries.[9]

Despite these discouraging signs, Small maintained his faith in the message of Simmelian sociology and professed his hope that the Spykman book would do "for Simmel and for social science what [the A/S] was unable to do thirty years ago" (Small 1925: 84). But Small's hopes for a sustaining Simmelian tradition were placed on the wrong source. While translations are necessary to the process of passing on European sociological traditions, they are not sufficient. Unless intellectual leaders make the translations come alive by drawing attention to their relevance to contemporary problems, those books and articles will likely lie fallow. For this reason, the American Simmelian tradition was not greatly advanced by Spykman's book, as Small had expected, but by members of his own department: by Robert E. Park in the years immediately following Small's leadership of the department, and by Everett C. Hughes later.[10]

Small played no minor role in this transition. It was Small, not W. I. Thomas, who first invited Park to Chicago, after they met one summer and spoke about Park's interests and German education. Small sensed a greater kinship with Park than Park did with Small, and the original offer was not accepted (Park n.d.: 2–3). But W. I. Thomas's subsequent and successful offer to Park after their meeting in 1912 surely required Small's sanction, as Hughes (1964: 18) would later intimate. After Park joined the faculty in 1914, he gathered about him most of the graduate students in the department with, again according to Hughes, "a strong supporting hand from Small" (Hughes 1953: 2). In addition, in one of his graduate seminars, Small translated with his students Park's Heidelberg doctoral thesis, "*Masse und Publicum*" (Hayner n.d.), and he had a hand in shaping the selections in Park and Burgess's text-reader, *Introduction to the Science of Society*. In particular, the curious absence of selections by Freud in the 1921 text, Raushenbush (1969: 2) reveals, was a result of Small's intervention. Small was in control, then, even as he transferred intellectual leadership of the department over to Park.

There was much in Park that Small would find congenial: his German Ph.D., his appreciation for German philosophy, his concern for society. But Park's acquaintance with Simmel and his knowledge of Simmel's writings must have been significant. Unlike Small, Park had studied with Simmel, his only formal instruction in sociology. In the winter semester of 1899–1900, in addition to courses with Paulsen and Frey, Park took Simmel's courses in ethics, sociology, and nineteenth-century philosophy. But this list of courses barely indicates the nature of what Hughes (1954b) called Park's "great indebtedness to Simmel." Others have begun to chart the extent of this debt. In addition to examining the Simmelian bearings of Park's dissertation (Levine 1972), researchers have examined Park's extension of Simmel's concepts, such as "social distance"; his appreciation of Simmel's essays, such as "The Stranger" (Levine 1985: 73–88); and the logical connections between Parkian and Simmelian social theory (Paharik 1983). But while these efforts examine theory in the service of sociology, they neglect to explore the role of theory in the service of society.

Consider the concept of interaction, a key term in Park's system and a nice rendering into English of Simmel's term "*Wechselwirkung*." Levine (1971: lii–liv) has done a service in identifying the theoretical and methodological implications of Park's extension of Simmel's term. But what were its social implications? What practical interest, what "drive for change," does the concept of interaction represent? A complete answer to this question would require a full-length study of Park's writings, beginning with the reformist impulses revealed in *Masse und Publicum* and ending with Park's final courses at Fisk University (Raushenbush 1979). Such a study, which will not be attempted here, would necessarily stress the role of "interaction" in Park's intellectual response to the turn-of-the-century problem of race adjustment or assimilation—the "Negro Problem."

From his earliest days as a newspaper reporter, including his muckraking journalism on King Leopold's Congo atrocities (Lyman 1992), to his work with Booker T. Washington at Tuskeegee Institute in Alabama, Park endeavored to improve the situation of people of color. His efforts embraced Washington's gradualist accommodationism, if not his boundless optimism, and rejected the fatalistic racialism of the times. These components of Park's practical agenda shaped his politics, his publications and his courses, including his first course at Chicago on "The Negro in America." As Park's lecture notes on "Interaction" show, the Simmelian term had a special part to play in this agenda.

Park's notes tell a story that turns on the device of contrasting old and new. In the past, Park reveals, scholars used to believe that the differences between people were "due to inherited differences; they were *racial* . . . [which] is to say they were fixed and immutable." But, he continued, these scholars' beliefs were shattered when they found that when people were "introduced into new environments" they behaved differently. In contrast to this earlier view, Park contends, "now we say 1) that different people develop the same institutions under similar circumstances; 2) that racial differences are not as great or as important as we suppose; and 3) that similar institutions and similar personality traits develop under similar conditions." Granting that certain temperamental differences exist between individuals and races, Park concluded, "After that we shall explain everything as the effect of interaction." Among the most decisive structural conditions shaping interaction, Park notes, is the size of the group. Here he links Simmel's essay on the influence of numbers to his own essay on "The City" (Park 1915), an essay which explores the consequences of urban life for social interaction.[11]

These notes add a new dimension to understanding the place of interaction in Park's system and his "great indebtedness" to Simmel. Like Small, who drew on Simmel to combat the outmoded and socially regressive doctrine of laissez faire, Park made Simmel central to his own practical interests and reform efforts. In a discussion of these efforts, Janowitz (1965: 733) noted: "Park, following on W. I. Thomas, was destroying biological racism and was searching for a new vocabulary of intergroup relations." Simmel's "interaction" was a part of this new vocabulary, providing Park with a "counter-concept" (Mannheim 1936: 272) to the outmoded racialist doctrines of the past. By focusing on interaction, Park shifted social analysis from an emphasis on inherent and immutable individual character-istics to social conditions and mutable personalities. The concep-tual turn was radical and nearly comprehensive. As Park noted, with few exceptions, such as the controversial notion of racial tempera-ment, "everything" can be explained by interaction. Rejecting the fatalism of racialist doctrine, this framework held open the promise that, through interaction and communication between peoples, racial accord could be reached. Along with the selections in *Intro-duction to the Science of Sociology*, it also provided a scientific rationale for the accommodationist approach to blacks in the Pro-gressive era.

Park and Burgess's *Introduction* (1st ed., 1921) was written in the aftermath of the 1919 summer race riots: in Washington, D.C., New York, Omaha, and Chicago, as well as throughout the South. In July of that year, a black swimmer crossed an invisible color line on one of Chicago's public beaches. He was killed by angry white men, and the subsequent three days of rioting left thirty-four dead, hundreds wounded, and several houses burned (Sandburg 1969 [1919]). Park (1923: 194) called the riot a "catastrophe" and "a sort of moral earthquake." If, according to one analyst, the riot expressed "a series of assaults upon the accommodative pattern by Negroes, indeed, a challenge to the very existence of that pattern" (Grimshaw 1959: 68), the *Introduction* provided a scientific defense of racial accommodation and an expression of hope in racial assimilation and accord. Extending Simmel's notion of interaction into "four great types"—competition, conflict, accommodation and assimilation—Park and Burgess turned the manifestations of urban discord into natural processes, as natural as the animal and plant life with which they were compared, with an evolutionary and progressive trend. The "final perfect product" (Park and Burgess 1969 [1921]: 736) of these four processes was assimilation, through which the bonds of a common cultural life would unite American citizens.

While Park held out the promise of assimilation for all, he was ambivalent about its prospects for blacks. As Lyman (1972) has shown, Park identified a number of troublesome obstacles—skin color, racial temperament, race prejudice, the absence of interracial intimacy—which, he believed, impeded the attainment of racial accord. Wherever he looked in contemporary America—in the North and the South, in urban and suburban regions—Park saw racial con-flict and accommodation, not assimilation. Curiously, it was in the past, during slavery, that Park found black and white unity: "By a curious paradox, slavery, and particularly household slavery, has probably been, aside from intermarriage, the most efficient device for promoting assimilation" (Park and Burgess 1969 [1921]: 739). The intimacy of contact between slaveholder and slave, he believed, reduced racial prejudice and fostered racial accommodation, a way of life shattered by emancipation and the ensuing racial strife.

In his romanticized view of slavery, in his views on racial temperament, which he never abandoned (see the discussion in Lyman 1992: 106–12; 119–20), and in his positive attitude toward racial accommodation, Park shared much with the Southern exponents of "racial accommodationism," Edgar Gardner Murphy and Benjamin F. Riley (Fredrickson 1971). Murphy, an Episcopal minister turned social reformer, was a close associate and supporter of Booker T. Washington. And Riley, a Baptist minister and author of The White Man's Burden, wrote an early and sympathetic biography of the black leader. Park was surely familiar with the writings of these men, who were so close to the Tuskegee leader that they have been called "white Washingtonians" (Fredrickson 1971: 293). Along with Nathan S. Shaler, a Northern popularizer of racial accommodationism and contributor to Park and Burgess's Introduction, these men battled the ascendant Negrophobia of the Jim Crow South with positive views of black character and support for racial cooperation. By portraying a rosy picture of slavery and promising racial unity through black accommodation to white society, their works found a receptive audience among Northern Progressives. While most of their ideas are outmoded and inaccurate, they were "enlightened" views for the time: optimistic and soothing to the white liberal conscience.

What Park added to this strain of Progressive thought was scientific legitimacy. He borrowed the term "accommodation" from James Mark Baldwin, the psychologist and moral philosopher, whose work, like his own, expressed a strong reaction against biological theories of society (Sewny 1967). Accommodation, a concept that was also an emergent value, assisted Baldwin in his own break with biological discourse. In his Dictionary of Philosophy and Psychology (1901–5), Baldwin distinguished between adaptation, a biological process of adjustment to the natural environment, and accommodation, a social and psychological process of adjustment to the social environment. On the basis of this distinction, Baldwin (1902) conceived a theory of individual development and social evolution which eschewed the Lamarckian principle of the inheritance of acquired characteristics. In place of this faulty principle, he proposed intelligent accommodative adjustments to the environment as a mechanism of advance, a view which had much in common with that of Lester F. Ward. Park found Baldwin's antibiological focus and his evolutionary progressivism compatible with his own beliefs. In the *Introduction*, he emphasized Baldwin's point that accommodations are socially and not biologically—that is, racially—transmitted: Social accommodations "are not a part of the racial inheritance of the individual, but are acquired by the person in social experience" (Park and Burgess 1969 [1921]: 664). And, like Baldwin, he regarded accommodation as a positive factor in social evolution, as it provided for a degree of relative equilibrium, a temporary stay of 'the war of all against all,' and a necessary phase before the peace and unity of assimilation.

Park also added a progressive component to racial accommodationism: Simmel's emphasis on reciprocity.[12] While Simmel's doctrine of reciprocity carries epistemological and ontological implications (e.g., Levine 1971), it also conveys ethical connotations. These implications vary depending on the context and subject under discussion. But one message that can be discerned may be described as a secularized manifestation of Christian reciprocal effect, such as is found in the Golden Rule: "Do as you would be done by." This ethical subtext underlies the *Introduction*'s Simmel selections, especially in those readings included under the category of "Accommodation," more than any other section[13] (see Table 2). Consider, for example, the important selection titled, "The Reciprocal Character of Subordination and Superordination," an excerpt from Small's translation of Simmel's essay "Superiority and Subordination."[14] When read along with the two essays that precede it—Münsterberg on "The Psychology of Subordination and Superordination," and "Memories of an Old Servant,"—the ethical import of Simmel's ideas become manifest.

"Society needs the leader as well as the followers," Münsterberg asserts, a sentiment shared by the three authors here under consideration (Park and Burgess 1969 [1921]: 690). But they also hold that leader and led have a reciprocal effect on each other. Münsterberg shows that just as the strong submit to the weak—through pity and the nobler altruistic sentiments, for example—so the weak lean on the strong. Everywhere, he argues, the weak "choose their actions under the influence of those in whom they have confidence." (p. 690) When, on the one hand, leaders inspire confidence, the led show feelings of modesty, admiration, gratitude, and hopefulness. When, on the other hand, leaders force submission, the led react with demonstrations of self-assertion: rejection, self-expression, and boast-

TABLE 2   Selected Chapters from *Introduction to the Science of Sociology* and Corresponding Simmel Selections

Social Contacts	Social Interaction	Competition	Conflict	Accommodation
The Sociological Significance of the "Stranger"*	"Social Interaction as the Definition of the Group in Time and Space"	"Money and Freedom"*	"Conflict as a Type of Social Interaction"	"The Reciprocal Character of Subordination and Superordination"
	"Sociology of the Senses: Visual Interaction"*		"Types of Conflict Situations"	"Three Types of Subordination and Superordination"
				"War and Peace as Types of Conflict and Accommodation"
				"Compromise and Accommodation"

Note: Selections marked with an asterisk were newly translated for the text-reader, while those with no asterisk were excerpted from Simmel's essays published in the *AJS* and translated by Albion Small. See Wolff (1950: lix) for more precise information on the source of these readings.

ful or pugnacious acts of self-display. The recollections of the anonymous "Old Servant" serve to exemplify Münsterberg's positive scenario. "Servants need a good example from their superiors," writes the author, "and when they hear the world speak well of them they do look for the good ways in the home life" (Park and Burgess 1969 [1921]: 693). The excerpt continues with a romanticized portrait of domestic service and a catalog of virtues allegedly following from close master-servant relationships: industry, deference, loyalty, honesty, earnestness, mutual respect.

Finally, the Simmel selection completes the moral lesson. While relationships between leaders and followers appears to be one-sided, with the one absolutely influencing and the other absolutely being influenced, in fact, Simmel argues, this is not the case. Behind the appearances there is a hidden and highly complex "reciprocal action of inferior upon superior" (Park and Burgess 1969 [1921]: 695). Indeed, relationships can be characterized by the degree of relative freedom and reciprocal action of the subordinate. Even under despotism, Simmel argues, subordinates have the right to press claims for reward or protection from the lawgiver. And "the monarch himself will be bound by the regulation which he has ordained" (p. 696). Such reciprocity between ruler and ruled was represented in Roman law, where "*lex*" implied both a ruler's promulgation of a decree and a subject's acceptance or rejection of it. Reciprocity between leader and led applies in modern societies, as well. Orator, teacher, journalist, politician—all seem to involve one-sided leadership. But the orator's assembly, the teacher's students, the journalist's audience, and the politician's public all limit and control the action of the leader. In summation, Simmel writes: "All leaders are also led, as in countless cases the master is the slave of his slaves" (p. 697).

In this selection, Simmel sets forth a positon on inequality whose ethical implications go beyond Münsterberg's and the old servant's implied support for racial paternalism. On the one hand, he concurs with them in the view that in relations with subordinates, leaders reap what they sow: "The decisive character of the relation [between superordinate and subordinate] . . . is this, that the effect which the inferior actually exerts upon the superior is determined by the latter" (Park and Burgess 1969 [1921]: 695). On the other hand, he goes beyond them in his arguments that the appearance of absolute control is deceptive, that the freedom of subordinates is a sociological given, that no human society or social group escapes reciprocal influence by subordinates, and that the rule of law provides rights as well as obligations. Taken together, these points support the position that dominance is always a two-way street, a negotiation beween leader and led. Also, when read in light of the racial conflicts of the Progressive era, they support an ethics of mutual dependence and accommodation between the races, of blacks and whites working together to live peacefully side by side.

SIMMEL AS INTELLECTUAL ROLE MODEL

In comparison to the many translations of Simmel's works by Small and Park, Everett C. Hughes's single published translation, "The Sociology of Sociability" (Simmel 1949), seems meager indeed. But it would be wrong to evaluate Hughes's impact on Simmel's American reception on the basis of this translation alone. After the death of his two teachers, and of Louis Wirth in 1952, Hughes was the hub around which much Simmel scholarship turned. Among the Simmel scholars of the period following World War II—Salomon at the New School, Merton at Columbia, for example—Hughes was *primus inter pares*.

His position as senior American Simmel scholar was part historical accident and part design. As a student in the mid-1920s of Small and Park, both of whom knew Simmel personally, Hughes later became the living link to the past. Certainly Merton could not claim such an aura; and Salomon's Heidelberg Ph.D. and writings on Weber resulted in his early identification as a representative of Weberian sociological thought (Johnson 1952: 343; Kalberg 1993).

But a more important reason for Hughes's significance is that he defined himself as a "Simmel man" (Hughes 1954a) and cultivated the study of Simmel at Chicago. Hughes's translation of the essay on "sociability," for example, was used in his classes to illustrate Simmel's understanding of the difference between "form" and "content" long before it was published in the *AJS* (Hughes 1971). And other untranslated sections of Simmel's *Soziologie* were regularly included in his lectures. Hughes's lectures and seminars on Simmel continued the Chicago Simmel tradition and inspired the next generation, including Hugh Dalziel Duncan, Erving Goffman, and Donald N. Levine. In contrast, there was no Simmel tradition at Columbia before Merton,[15] whose involvement with Simmel was fertile but unsustained (Jaworski 1990); and Salomon turned his attention and sympathies to French social thought after the war (Salomon 1955).

Consequently, as senior American Simmel scholar, Hughes's opinion about matters Simmelian was regularly sought and his influence was widespread. This is shown especially in his behind-the-scenes role in the postwar Simmel translations. When in 1947 Hughes was approached by Jeremiah Kaplan, the twenty-year-old cofounder of The Free Press, about translating Simmel, he recommended Kurt H. Wolff, whom he had met several years earlier during Wolff's postdoctoral study at Chicago.[16] Wolff included an acknowledgment to Hughes in *The Sociology of Georg Simmel* (1950), his translation of parts of Simmel's *Soziologie* and a few other pieces. Later, when Kaplan wanted additional translations, Hughes read and made suggestions for improving the text of *Conflict and the Web of Group Affiliations*, translated by Wolff and Reinhard Bendix, and he wrote a foreword to the volume (Hughes 1955). During President Johnson's "War on Poverty," when a translation of Simmel's essay "The Poor" was being published, Hughes reviewed the manuscript and wrote a prefatory note to the translation, "A Note on Georg Simmel" (Hughes 1965).

The "Note" is characteristic of Hughes's writings on Simmel, brief and filled with tantalizing hints about his interest in the German sociologist. One such clue is his characterization of Simmel as "a man both extraordinarily humane and extraordinarily detached, a complete liberal intellectual" (Hughes 1965: 117). One senses that in Simmel Hughes found an intellectual role model: not as a theorist to slavishly follow—for Hughes read Simmel not for knowledge but for inspiration—but as a man whose intellectual style he found appealing.[17] Urbane and erudite, Simmel could analyze profound matters while writing on apparently frivolous topics. Hughes contrasts the sober scholarship of Weber to the playful style of Simmel in a manner that reflects, perhaps, more personal differences between himself and his two real-life role models: his father, the Methodist minister, and his mentor Robert Park, the newspaperman-turned-sociologist.

> At the first meeting of the German Sociological Society in 1910, Max Weber proposed a program of study of two current phenomena—voluntary associations and the newspaper. Simmel gave a gala opening address on the apparently frivolous topic of the "Sociology of Sociability," taking as one of his illustrations décolleté dress which has the double function of exciting men to playful mood while keeping them at a distance. Weber was speaking as secretary at a business session; Simmel was introducing sociology to the élite of intellectual Frankfurt. Each was perfectly cast. (Hughes 1965: 117)

Hughes once wrote that in matters of personal and intellectual style, he was "more of a Simmel than a Weber man" (Hughes 1954a). While Hughes was interested in much of what Simmel wrote, I believe that "The Sociology of Sociability," his only published Simmel translation, is emblematic of what he found most compelling in Simmel. An analysis of some of the arguments in Simmel's essay helps to elucidate not only Hughes's affinities to Simmel, but also what may have been the strategic aims of publishing his translation when he did. Published in 1949, the bicentennial year of Goethe's birth, the essay manifests Hughes's belief in the enduring significance of Western spiritual values. Used regularly in his classes throughout the forties—during the Nazi imperilment of democracy and the domestic pressures of wartime—Simmel's essay offered wise counsel during dark times.

WORLD CRISIS AND THE REDEMPTIVE VALUE OF SOCIABILITY

Simmel's essay on sociability characteristically analyzes the larger social significance of an interactional form. Here he discusses sociable conversations—in courtly society and in the salons of his acquaintance—and finds in them a microcosm of contemporary social ideals. The rules of sociability exclude personal and substantive concerns from the conversational game; or, at least, if one discusses such matters they are treated lightly, playfully, and artfully. When such everyday concerns as gaining and losing advantage are excluded from sociable conversation, the single goal of mutual joy could be realized. To quote Simmel (1949: 257):

> Sociability creates, if one will, an ideal sociological world, for in it—so say the enunciated principles—the pleasure of the individual is always contingent upon the joy of others; here by definition, no one can have his satisfaction at the cost of contrary experiences on the part of others.

This temporary equality of sociability thus symbolically manifests the possibility and promise of democracy:

> This world of sociability, the only one in which a democracy of equals is possible without friction, is an *artificial* world, made up of beings who have renounced both the objective and the purely personal features of the intensity and extensiveness of life in order to bring about among themselves a pure interaction, free of any disturbing material accent. (Simmel 1949: 257)

But sociable conversation does more than symbolically fulfill democracy's promise. Like nature and art, it serves a redemptive function, what Simmel called "a saving grace and blessing effect" (Simmel 1949: 261). Because sociability frees us, if momentarily, from our cares and provides a "saving exhilaration" in talk, modern men and women are able to bear the weight of life's burdens and agitations. "The whole weight of life," Simmel's essay concludes, "is [in sociability] consumed in an artistic play, in that simultaneous sublimation and dilution, in which the heavily freighted forces of reality are felt only as from a distance, their weight fleeting in a charm" (Simmel 1949: 261).

This view of the redeeming possibilities of conversation provided a fitting vision not only for Simmel's salon society, but also for the American academy during rising fears of communist menace in American educational institutions.[18] The image of conversation as democratic and redemptive offered a liberal counterimage to paranoid suspicions of subversive conversation on academic campuses. It was a timely message, sent during the year in which an anticommunist witch hunt at Chicago was resoundingly defeated. From 1947 to 1949 the Broyles Commission, an Illinois State anti-Communist crusade, "focussed on education, and on the University of Chicago in particular" (Schrecker 1986: 113). In a series of public hearings in the spring of 1949, faculty and administrators were confronted with supposedly incriminating evidence against them. Among those questioned was Ernest W. Burgess, the Sociology Department Chairman, who defended himself against allegations that he was affiliated with a communist 'front' organization (Harsha 1952 [1949]: 118 ff). The Broyles Commission was unsuccessful, finding no Communists on the faculty—a result due in no small measure to the defiant attitude toward the Commission's activities on the part of University Chancellor Robert Hutchins and many university professors. Hughes's translation played no known instrumental role in this action; but it can be read today as symbolic of the resistance.

But the optimism manifest in Simmel's vision of the redemptive possibilities of sociability was tempered by a darker message expressed in his essay, the recognition of the inherent fragility of "pure" forms. This point is expressed in the translation when Simmel acknowledges that sociability "may easily get entangled with real life" (Simmel 1949: 258). It is to this message that Hughes would turn later in life when he had occasion to reflect on Simmel's sociology:

> The idea in [Simmel's] paper on sociability is an interesting one. The notion that there can be a social interaction completely as a play form without any ulterior goal. He makes indeed by implication the point that it is very hard to keep it unsullied. I think it is hard to keep any kind of interaction unsullied by other forms or ulterior goals. (Hughes 1970: 3)

Hughes expresses here a view of a corrupted or failed humanity, a view expressed in his wartime writings on the failed realization of Western ideals. Instead of justice he witnessed vilification; instead of equality he saw exclusion; and instead of truth he found compromise and rationalization (e.g., Hughes 1945; 1952 [1947]; 1963 [1943]). But, if Simmel's essay gave support to Hughes's sense of a corrupted humanity, it also showed how scholarship might proceed under such conditions: with good humor rather than heavy seriousness; with an attention to large processes in small phenomena. Hughes and Simmel were both humanists trying to craft an improbable science during treacherous times. Simmel's essay on sociability showed how this can be done. He discovered democracy in a teacup, redemption from life's distress over lunch, and truth in a low-cut dress.[19]

CONCLUSION

I set out to reveal the ways in which Simmel's reception by three Chicago sociologists contributed to contemporary discourse on moral and political issues. This goal was formed in response to recent concerns that sociology has failed to make significant contributions to civic discourse. By documenting the moral and political orientations of key figures in sociology, I have attempted not only to uncover the past, but to provide models for the future.

To recognize this feature of the American reception of Simmel's work is not to deny that there were good intellectual reasons for an interest in Simmel. One can and must examine the historical and contemporary interest in Simmel from both points of view. Indeed, it is probably an error to consider theoretical reason and practical life as polar terms. A pragmatic and phenomenologically informed study of social theory, its production and reception, would explore the links between life world and social thought. But the main justification for this one-sided portrait of the early American Simmel translations is that it provides a needed balance to past studies, which neglect to study translators' practical interests and moral concerns.

Typically, discussions of translations in sociology take one of two strategies. They may, first, feature the technical aspects of translation, for example, by discussing word choice and special translation difficulties (e.g., Gerth and Mills 1958 [1946]; Wolff 1950); or, they may, second, study the "Americanization" of an author's writings, studying the shifts in meaning that result from transmission into an American context of works written, say, in a German context (e.g., Hinkle 1986; Roth 1992). In contrast to these approaches, I have studied translations as strategic resources in contests over moral or political issues. The selection of texts, the timing of publication, the translation of words and ideas, the interpretation of meaning—all may be considered as possible elements in sociologists' engagement with social issues, as forms of social action. If translations serve intellectual needs, I have suggested, they may also serve moral and political purposes. Future research along these lines might profit by pursuing a synthesis of this distinctive approach with the more conventional ways of studying translations. A complete examination of efforts to translate Simmel into the American idiom would require such an analysis of the technical, cultural, and practical aspects of the transmission.

My main contribution, however, has been to tell the story of the American Simmel reception, or at least one significant part of it, as a chapter in the continuing struggle to define America. Read in this way, the translations and discussions of Simmel's writings tell a story of scholar-citizens struggling to shape the prevailing definitions of human behavior and society: of Small battling the inhumanity of laissez faire capitalism; of Park creating a new language to replace the dangerous ranting of biological racism; of Hughes offering a commentary on American society troubled by domestic and world crisis. If these efforts fail to meet strictly scientific standards, they may be read with different standards in mind. There is much in them to be admired. They demonstrate courage in the face of adversity, passion in the pursuit of truth, and vigor in the effort to guide America through stormy times.

CHAPTER 2

PARK, DOYLE, AND HUGHES: NEGLECTED ANTECEDENTS OF GOFFMAN'S THEORY OF CEREMONY

Efforts to systematize Erving Goffman's sociological contributions are under way (see Chriss 1995). In addition, two major exegetical studies of Goffman have recently been published (Burns 1992; Manning 1992) and more such studies are expected. Since these efforts are proliferating, it might be prudent to take stock of just what Goffman's contributions are. In what ways is he original, in what ways conventional, in what ways right or wrong? Without answers to these questions, scholars may not only render unto Goffman what is not properly his, but do a disservice to contemporary sociological inquiry as well. Efforts to move "beyond Goffman" (Riggins 1990) may fail unless we understand his work in relation to the Chicago tradition that he absorbed and extended.

In this chapter, I examine Goffman's work on etiquette and front—his theory of ceremony—with an eye to these concerns. My purpose is to discover his contributions to this area against the backdrop of the tradition of inquiry within which those contributions were made. While other topics could have been selected, the focus on ceremony has a number of virtues. Etiquette and front are central to Goffman's writings, allowing for close comparison of texts and an analysis of the ways Goffman conforms to the assumptions of his forebears and the ways he departs from them. Moreover, the available studies of Goffman's approach to ceremonial observances (e.g., Bovone 1993; Strong 1988) offer much exegesis but little contextual analysis of Goffman's ideas. Such studies often manifest the "Columbus complex" identified by Sorokin (1965), the erroneous belief that contemporary scholars are the discoverers of what are actually well-troden fields of inquiry. In contrast, my analysis situates Goffman's writings within the Chicago tradition of Robert E. Park, Bertram W. Doyle, and Everett C. Hughes. These neglected antecedents are crucial to understanding Goffman's own work.[1] Indeed, Goffman's debt to these men pervades his work, going well beyond that which can be discussed in a single essay; but it is here that this debt can begin to be documented.

The following analysis begins with a review of selected findings from previous investigations into Goffman's intellectual biography. The second section discusses major facets of the Chicago School tradition of studies on etiquette and front. The third section analyzes the development of Goffman's writings on these subjects. Together, this analysis reveals the ways in which Goffman's work presents a creative synthesis and extension of the various strains in this literature. A conclusion discusses Goffman's creativity, the intellectual constraints on his originality, and the implications of these for future studies of etiquette.

On Goffman's Intellectual Genealogy

Goffman's disinclination to situate himself within a theoretical heritage or tradition frustrates current efforts to establish his intellectual genealogy. He rebuked those who would attempt to tie him down to one tradition or approach (Goffman 1981; Verhoeven 1993), and he rejected the term symbolic interactionism, the intellectual movement with which he was often associated. Some researchers have sought to compensate for these difficulties by examining Goffman's citations, believing that this practice would yield answers to questions of influential figures (MacCannell 1983; Hettlage and Lenz 1991; Smith 1989: 431–44). Others (Verhoeven 1993; Winkin 1984) who could ask Goffman himself, have published their revealing interviews. Still others have offered creative reconstructions of the stages of Goffman's intellectual development (Collins 1981 [1979]). Yet, however rich and varied the influences on Goffman may have been, the literature continues to point to the intellectual centrality of Goffman's Chicago years.[2]

Consider the citation analyses.[3] One early study (MacCannell 1983), which limited its analysis to *Presentation of Self*, found a preponderance of references to the French philosopher Jean Paul Sartre. Later and more extensive investigations have expanded this picture. Examining a range of Goffman's writings, a German scholar found, as Coser recently noted, that Everett C. Hughes "is cited as often as Georg Simmel and almost as often as Emile Durkheim" (Coser 1994:

10). Smith's (1989: 212) analysis of references to Simmel in Goffman's work provides an additional insight. Nearly two-thirds of those citations occur by 1956, that is, in the writings deriving from Goffman's Chicago years. Two separate interviews with Goffman, conducted in 1980 and published later, confirm the importance of Goffman's Chicago years. In an interview with Yves Winkin (1984: 236), Goffman stated: "I was formed by Hughes and *Presentation of Self* is really in the Hughesian tradition of structural social psychology." Moreover, Goffman reportedly referred to Hughes as his "patron saint" at Chicago (Winkin 1988: 35). In Verhoeven's interview, Goffman adds another name: Robert Park. Goffman notes that Park "was sort of the founder of the whole Hughesian tradition. He had a lot of influence on us I think. My teachers were Park, Burgess, and Louis Wirth. And then later on Everett Hughes" (Verhoeven 1993: 321). Since Park died a year before Goffman began studies at Chicago, he could not have meant that Park was his classroom teacher; but Burgess was alive and still teaching from his classic treatise written with Park, *Introduction to the Science of Sociology* (1969 [1921]).

Goffman situates himself, then, in a tradition founded by Park and Burgess and modified by Hughes. Citation studies confirm the significance of Simmel to Goffman's early work (see also, Smith 1994 [1989]). But what tradition links Goffman to Park, Hughes and Simmel? An analysis of a related question by Winkin (1988: 36–41) points toward the moral, methodological, and thematic continuities in their work. Morally, he detects the transmission and attenuation of the Social Gospel from Park to Hughes to Goffman; methodologically, he finds the persistence of the fieldwork tradition; thematically, he sees continuities in the study of urban life. My review of their writings reveals additional thematic continuities on another analytical plane. Goffman's various discussions of "front" drew on a Chicago school tradition of research on social accommodation, etiquette, and front, a literature that formed a nascent sociology of everyday life. While a full analysis of this intellectual tradition cannot be offered here, a discussion of its main outlines provides a basis for indentifying Goffman's unique contributions to the tradition.

Etiquette as Control and Mask: Spencerian and Simmelian Strains in Robert Park's Social Theory

Social accommodation is one of the "four great types" of interaction identified in Park and Burgess's *Introduction*. Articulating a model later called the "race relations cycle," the classic textbook shows how contact between peoples leads inevitably to *competition* and *conflict*, then to *accommodation*, the temporary working adjustment to those antagonisms, and finally to *assimilation*, or cultural and personal unification. Park and his students spent years studying race relations around the world from this perspective (see Lyman 1972). But accommodation has a more general significance in Park's work than is suggested by its specific association with the study of race. It provides a key to Park's understanding of the social order (Turner 1967).

Park borrowed the term "accommodation" from James Mark Baldwin, the psychologist and moral philosopher, whose work, like his own, expressed a strong reaction against biological theories of society (Sewny 1967). In his *Dictionary of Philosophy and Psychology* (1901–1905), Baldwin distinguished between adaptation, a biological process of adjustment to the natural environment, and accommodation, a social and psychological process of adjustment to the social environment. By adopting this term, Park was rejecting such answers to the problem of social order as "common will," "identity of interests," "imitation," and so on, in favor of a social and evolutionary answer. Just as the geological record displays the adaptations of the species to its changing natural environment, so the historical record reveals the accommodations, in custom and the mores, to the changing social environment.[4]

Etiquette provides one clue to understanding the social adjustments in personal relations reached in any one historical era. In a world of social and personal differences, of mutual antagonisms and antipathies, etiquette operates as both "a principle of social order and an index of the stability of the society in which it exists" (Park 1950 [1937]: 183). It originates, Park believed, in the spontaneous expression of social sentiment—of deference and recognition—of one person in the presence of another, and is modified into the social ritual of obligatory expression called etiquette. By so defining the proper distances and degrees of social respect, etiquette represents a temporary agreement to suspend social conflict and to get on with the requirements of social life.

As social relations change, as the arrangements of wealth, power and prestige alter through social change and individual effort, the social rituals no longer manifest common sentiments; then they serve, to quote Park (1950 [1937]: 183),

> as the masque behind which one controls and conceals his emotions rather than reveals them. Etiquette in that case becomes a social device by which one does the expected thing but preserves his inner freedom.

Such a social device is commonly called a "front." Park and Burgess (1969 [1921]: 732) directed the readers of their *Introduction* to study fronts, calling on them to investigate "the Subtler Forms of Accommodation: Flattery, 'Front,' Ceremony, etc."

Park's own writings on etiquette drew on the work of Herbert Spencer and Georg Simmel. Park (1950 [1937]: 182) specifically mentions his "indebtedness" to Herbert Spencer. Montaigne may have preceeded Spencer in underscoring the pervasiveness of ceremony, but it was Spencer's discussion of "ceremonial observance" in his *Principles of Sociology* that made etiquette a legitimate subject of sociological investigation.[5] According to Spencer, etiquette was a form of social government or social control. Indeed, it was an early and pervasive form of social control, and "still [had] 'the largest share in regulating men's lives'" (Park 1950 [1937]: 182). It operates, Park notes, by assigning people a "place" in society and defining social distances. Forms of address, ceremonies of deference, lists of dos and don'ts—all regulate social life by reproducing the dominant hierarchies. As long as people keep in their place and maintain their proper distances, open social conflict is avoided and stability is achieved.

If Spencer's discussion of "ceremonial observances" directed attention to the functions of etiquette for social stability, Simmel's theory of the autonomization and ossification of social forms provided Park with a different lesson. It offered a model for Park's discussion of the natural history of etiquette: from living expression of social sentiments to mask or front. As Simmel (1949) explains in his essay on "Sociability," the actual forces, needs and impulses of life produce the forms of culture and social interaction. Through time, these forms become autonomous from their roots and valued in their own right irrespective of their expressive value. Such autonomous forms can ossify, losing their connection to the human purposes for which they were created. Then art, for example, becomes artifice and play becomes 'empty play' (Simmel 1949: 43). Extending this perspective to an analysis of the *ancien regime*, Simmel drew attention to the hollow and superficial character of courtly etiquette. When courtly etiquette became valued in its own right, it "no longer referred to any content" (Simmel 1949: 56) and became an empty form.

Bertram W. Doyle followed the Spencerian strain in Park's thinking when writing his study, *The Etiquette of Race Relations in the South: A Study in Social Control* (Doyle 1937).[6] Doyle portrays etiquette as an elementary, universal, and effective form of social control. He expresses a clear dissatisfaction with the legal solutions to racial conflict proposed by the many racial commissions of the time. These legal solutions fail to consider elementary sociological wisdom, which reveals that custom is more effective than law in controlling social conduct. To quote Doyle: When "the Negro . . . [is] in doubt as to what is expected of him, he will ask what is customary—not what is the law" (Doyle 1937: 161). Since the old codes of conduct between blacks and whites were dissolving, new forms of etiquette, more than new laws, were needed to ease contemporary racial tensions. This is the dominant practical message of the book. It was an argument that encouraged racial accommodation rather than racial justice; it encouraged social adjustment to a system of inequality rather than the dismantling of that system. As McKee (1993: 151) notes, Doyle's argument was comforting to those in power, since it "provided assurance that race relations were only slowly changing and that most blacks had no serious expectations of [social change]."

Doyle shared the assumption with Park that social inequality and social distance were necessary to the smooth functioning of society. The penultimate chapter of the book quotes Park favorably on this point:

> While etiquette and ceremonial are at once a convenience and a necessity in facilitating human discourse, they serve even more effectively to preserve the rank and order of individuals and classes, which seems to be essential to social organization and effective social action. (Park quoted in Doyle 1937: 171)

By holding this assumption, Park and Doyle misinterpreted the thought of Herbert Spencer, whom they regularly cited to sanction their belief. In contrast to the Chicago sociologists, Spencer explicitly established a relationship between etiquette and political power. In Spencer's terminology, there was a connection between ceremony and militancy. "Ceremony," he wrote, "originates from *fear*: on the one side, supremacy of a victor or master; on the other side, dread of death or punishment felt by the vanquished or slave" (Spencer 1969 [1882]: 167). Moreover, since militant societies give way to industrial societies, so ceremonial observances, which become increasingly repugnant as the range of freedoms enlarges, pass away or transform into rules of mutual politeness (p. 173). While Spencer warned against the "premature decay of ceremonial rule" (p. 174), he was quick to point out that progress would ensure the gradual "disuse of obeisance, of complimentary forms of address, of titles, of badges, etc." None of these ideas found their way into the views of Park

and Doyle, who elided the analysis of etiquette and racial domination and insisted not on the withering away of racial etiquette, as in
Spencer, but on its persistence.

From their revisionist point of view, freedom for the Negro
will be found within this system of ranking, not by transcending
the system. Park located inner freedom behind the accommodating
mask of etiquette. Doyle discovered it in a stance of critical detachment toward the existing codes of etiquette, a view that anticipates
Goffman's notion of "role distance." The person who is detached
from the codes, Doyle argues, neither defends nor decries existing
conditions. Such a person may or may not be placed in a situation
where he or she is expected to abide by those codes. If this person
does use them, "he plays at the practice, as at an amusing game." In
this *playing at* etiquette, as opposed to playing it straight, lies "the
true emancipation of the Negro" (Doyle 1937: 168).

If Doyle followed the Spencerian strain in Park's thinking,
Everett C. Hughes followed the Simmelian line.[7] He directed his
students to study the empty fronts of social life—especially those
presented by modern organizations. There was a biographical basis to
this intellectual preference. By his own account, Hughes was part of
a generation that revolted against the formalism of etiquette and
ceremony. This was, he wrote, "a well-meaning generation who
believed that all good things could be attained by science and all
bad things avoided by emancipation from old formulae and freedom
from old distinctions; the people who got it into their heads that
anything formal is cold" (Hughes 1958 [1952]: 16). The basis for this
revolt, he maintained, was a faith "in progress, in things getting better and better" (p. 17). Such a belief, Hughes came to realize, ignored
not only the cycles of social life but the benefits of the repeated rites
that ease movement through those cycles. An important layer of
human protection and defense was lost when people forgot "that
ceremonial may be the cloak that warms the freezing heart; that a
formula may be the firm stick upon which the trembling limbs may
lean; that it may be a house in which one may decently hide himself" (p. 17).

Etiquette and ceremony serve a defensive function for individuals: they shield the soul from exposure. This is not their purpose in
modern soulless organizations. Corporations and other large organizations employ ceremony and front to shield naked self-interest.
These groups readily adopt the ceremonial forms that the individuals
of Hughes's generation too quickly abandoned. According to Hughes,
"when an occupation develops its own institution for control of [an]
occupation, and protection of its prerogatives, it is likely to develop

what we may call a culture, an etiquette, and a group within which one may attain the satisfaction of his wishes" (Hughes 1971 [1928]: 337). Hughes mentions as examples, first, the quasi-religious order of the Chicago Real Estate Board and, second, the tycoons of the turn-of-the-century, who developed a set of practices and an etiquette "for their protection" (p. 335).

Recognizing that etiquette served organizations as a protection racket—"a body of ritual that grows up informally to preserve, before the clients, the common front of the profession" (Hughes 1939: 273)—Hughes devised a research strategy to see through these fronts. As Simpson (1972: 548) notes, Hughes directed his students to study firsthand the lowly professions and institutions, for "[such groups] are less able to clothe themselves with cultural elaborations to shield their inner workings." In Hughes's seminar on "Work and Occupations," Goffman was directed to conduct an ethnographic study of such an occupation. This research resulted in his first publication, "Symbols of Class Status" (Goffman 1951). The discussion of "curator groups" in that essay was developed further in subsequent research, such as in the unpublished report on "The Service Station Dealer" (Goffman 1953b) written for Lloyd Warner; and again in *Presentation*, where such occupations are described as "service specialists" (Goffman 1959: 153–59). Goffman continued to study such people, for they were natural Hughesian sociologists whose jobs positioned them to see behind the multiple masks of the modern bourgeoisie. In Goffman's words, "They learn the secrets of the show" (Goffman 1959: 153).

GOFFMAN ON CEREMONIAL OBSERVANCES

Goffman's writings on ceremonial observances synthesize the Spencerian and Simmelian strands in the Chicago literature on etiquette. On the one hand, he departed from Hughes's belief in the erosion of ceremony in everyday life by affirming the centrality of those ceremonies. In this respect, Goffman shared with Park and Doyle the Spencerian perspective on ceremonial observances. His kinship with those forebears is witnessed in the frontispiece to *Relations in Public* (1971). There he reproduces in full the quotation from Spencer's *Principles of Sociology* referenced above, the same passage Park and Doyle were fond of quoting:

If, disregarding conduct that is entirely private, we consider only that species of conduct which involves direct relations with other persons; and if under the name of government we include all control of such conduct, however arising; then we must say that the earliest kind of government, and the government which is ever spontaneously recommencing, is the government of ceremonial observances. More may be said. This kind of government, besides preceding other kinds, and besides having in all places and times approached nearer to universality of influence, has ever had, and continues to have, the largest share in regulating men's lives.

Other indications of Goffman's participation in Park's line of research include his interactionist interpretation of Park's term "accommodation." In Park's writings discussed above, accommodation denotes those social arrangements that suspend social conflict and facilitate social interaction. Such arrangements enable members of a society or group to live and work on friendly terms. Accommodation does not mean total agreement on all essentials, but a *modus vivendi*, a temporary accord that may permit, in Park's view, a more complete unification.

Goffman shifted the analytical focus of the term from Park's macrolevel of analysis to a situational level. In doing so, he was making explicit a dimension of the term left implicit in Park's own writings.[8] In *Presentation*, for example, Goffman writes of interactants forming a "working consensus" and developing a kind of "interactional *modus vivendi*" (Goffman 1959: 9). An agreement to "avoid open conflict" is made in exchange for the smooth accomplishment of situational goals. Echoing the Simmelian origins of the term, Goffman (1959: 10) underscored the variability of content and generality of form of these working arrangements. Another instructive contrast might be found in Goffman's essay on "Face Work" (Goffman 1967 [1955]: 5–45), which extends to everyday life the analysis of courtesy and etiquette in international race relations found in Park's important essay, "Behind Our Masks" (Park 1926). In these writings, Goffman took the study of etiquette and 'front' beyond his predecessors. No longer confined to the study of race relations or the professions, etiquette would inform studies of social interaction generally.

On the other hand, he followed Hughes in working from the Simmelian strain in Park's social theory. For both Hughes and Goffman, etiquette was no longer the living expression of common social sentiments; it had ossified into a "front," an obligatory and restricting expression of social rank. If Hughes studied institutional fronts, Goffman emphasized individual fronts (Cf. Helmes-Hayes 1994: 31).

While Goffman often varied his terms, sometimes referring to 'line' and other times to 'role' or 'front,' his early writings emphasize the difficulties modern men and women encounter with the masks they are required to wear. He contends that social roles become institutionalized and confining, and that there are too few of them to allow for the expression of social complexity and diversity. Writing of these issues in "On Face Work," he postulates that "a small choice of lines" (Goffman 1967 [1955]: 7), conventionalized courses of conduct, are available to modern men and women. The standardization and economy of fronts pose problems for social actors, who are forced to make uncertain choices among them. Illustrating these problems in *Presentation*, he discusses how nurses who perform advanced medical tasks are obliged to act in a subordinate role or risk making an affront; hostesses for the same reason must carefully decide the degree of formality for dress and table; and intellectual entrepreneurs must avoid the appearance of being an upstart by wrapping their new ideas in old packaging (Goffman 1959: 27–29).[9] Like actors in a repertory company with a limited wardrobe, modern men and women are forced to wear anachronistic or otherwise inappropriate costumes. They do so for the benefits gained by appearing moral in our society, and with the fear and trepidation of potential failure.

When in his essay on "Role Distance" Goffman (1961b) turned again to etiquette and front, he did so in a different spirit and with quite different results. If, in *Presentation* and other early writings, Goffman portrayed fronts as determining social action and expression, and individuals as fatalistically adopting them, in "Role Distance" he explicitly rejected this determinism:

> When we get closer to the moment-to-moment conduct of the individual we find that he does not remain passive in face of the potential meanings that are generated regarding him, but, so far as he can, actively participates in sustaining a definition of the situation that is stable and consistent with his image of himself. (Goffman 1961b: 104)

Developing a point earlier anticipated by Doyle, but apparently discovered independently, Goffman points out that individuals don't just *play roles*, they also *play at* roles, or exert other "creative acts of distancy" (Goffman 1961b: 108).[10] Such stylized role playing reverses, or "gives full twist to," what Goffman calls "the iron law of etiquette":

> The act through which one can afford to try to fit into the situation is an act that can be styled to show that one is some-

what out of place. One enters a situation to the degree that one can demonstrate that one does not belong. (Goffman 1961b: 109)

In addition to his well-known example of age-graded behavior on the merry-go-round, Goffman illustrates role distance by discussing medical etiquette and the ways in which surgeons, especially, abide by the obligations while also ridiculing them (he uses the theatrical slang term *guy*). One example will suffice here:

> This body of custom [of medical etiquette] requires that the surgeon, on leaving the operation, turn and thank his assistant, his anesthetist, and ordinarily his nurses as well. Where a team has worked together for a long time and where the members are of the same age-grade, the surgeon may guy this act, issuing the thanks in what he expects will be taken as an ironical and farcical tone of voice: "Miss Westly, you've done a simply wonderful job here." (Goffman 1961b: 119)

The term "role distance" has functionalist roots. While Coser (1956a) was developing his Simmelian theory of "safety-valve institutions," Hughes was exploiting the same ideas at a different level of analysis. He coined the term "role release" (see Goffman 1961a: 94, note 165) to refer to those occasions in which one is "released" from the customary role expectations and allowed to act differently. By allowing for the controlled catharsis of pent-up hostilities, resentments or tensions, such occasions and acts serve the latent function of contributing to social order.

Goffman's new term "role distance" offerred a conceptual extension of Hughes's notion while incorporating Merton's language of latent functions. His essays present what might be called an "interactionist functionalism." To cite just one example, Goffman maintains that acts of role distance, such as the surgeon's farcical line cited above, can provide "functionally useful relaxations" (Goffman 1961b: 124). In this view, role distance contributes to social order by reducing the tensions in the workplace, such as in the above example of the hospital's high-stress environment.[11] Other examples could be cited. Later, in *Frame Analysis* (1974), Goffman would retain the functionalist terminology, but shorn of the mechanistic tension-release formula presented earlier. "The function of a striking remark, ironic, witty or learned, is . . . to generate the notion that an interactant brings a personage along with him" (Goffman 1974: 299). The conception that we have personalities beyond or apart from our roles, Goffman now maintains, constitutes a cognitive condition of social order. It provides an underlying sense of continuity among our diverse doings. In this study, functionalist analysis is extended in poststructuralist directions.

If role distance contributes to social solidarity, it does so in a way that may satisfy individuals' efforts to subvert that order. This feature of role distance comes out in the discussion of front in *Asylums*, especially in the section on institutional display and ceremonies (Goffman 1961a: 93–112). Goffman does not yet use the term role distance, but he discusses its features *avant la lettre*. Goffman noted that in many total institutions, staff and inmates together engage in periodic activities that symbolize, to themselves and outside audiences, the unity or solidarity of the institution. Such activities—the production of house newsletters, theatrical performances, open houses, and the like—reverse the more routine course of activities, which acts to separate staff and inmates. As such, these occasional activities serve as a front for the indignities of daily institutional life. They also provide subordinates with the opportunity to "act out" their rebellion, turning their conspiracy, which might otherwise undermine the organization, into expression, which satisfies individual and institution alike (Goffman 1961a: 110). Goffman notes that "there is often a hint or a splash of rebellion in the role that inmates take in these [institutional] ceremonies. Whether through a sly article, a satirical sketch, or overfamiliarity during a dance, the subordinate in some way profanes the superordinate" (p. 109). Goffman argues that persons do not only take roles, they also actively alter their expression, and often in subversive ways (cf. Turner 1962).

In *Presentation of Self*, Goffman portrays a world where fronts were merely selected and, depending on the choice, either suffered or enjoyed. That deterministic worldview—represented in the stoical Protestantism that shaped Park's sense of etiquette—Goffman abandons in his later writings. In those later publications, he describes a world in which roles are *played at*, acts are *guyed*, and the iron law of etiquette is given *a full twist*. All of these notions emphasize the relative freedom of a person from a role. Goffman's notion of the person also loosens; it is to be found in little more than personal style. Consider the final comments to "Role Distance," Goffman's answer to the emerging romanticism of the encounter group generation. He took the opportunity in those pages to criticize efforts to "keep a part of the world safe from sociology" (Goffman 1961b: 152), such as by searching for authentic selfhood in lives separated from social roles. On the contrary, shedding social roles will provide no benefit, Goffman holds; it is through playing with roles, through role distance, "that the individual's personal style is to be found" (Goffman 1961b: 152). Both Park's advice to preserve inner freedom behind the accommodating mask of etiquette, and the encounter movement's advice to shed social masks in favor of natural selves, are here rejected and replaced by Goffman's advice to play our parts, but in our own unique style.

CONCLUSION

Goffman's contributions to the theory of ceremony were forged within a Chicago tradition of inquiry on etiquette and front. Above all, it was Robert Park's attention to etiquette and other ceremonial observances that formed Goffman's 'horizon of understanding' on these matters (Gadamer 1975 [1965]: 302 ff). As I have shown, Park's writings provided a perspective and a line of inquiry that drew on both Spencer and Simmel. His work, and the work of his students Doyle and Hughes, addressed many issues Goffman would later take up: self, role, 'front', ceremony, morality, social order. It is necessary to identify Goffman's conributions to these areas within the context of this neglected Chicago tradition if future research is to avoid the pitfalls of granting Goffman too much, or of granting him too little. Goffman is granted too much when researchers attribute to him the discovery of insights or conceptual distinctions that were actually articulated by others. He is granted too little when his real contributions are left uncovered for want of adequate contextual analysis. Examining Goffman in context shows how much he owes to others; but, it also shows how he moved beyond them. The above analysis reveals that Goffman's contribution to the theory of ceremony was a synthesis of the diverse strands embodied in Park's social theory and advanced by Doyle and Hughes in different directions.

If Goffman advanced this tradition of inquiry on etiquette and front, he also was constrained by it. It was the belief that fronts are necessary to social life—to ensure social order (Park, Doyle), to preserve inner freedom (Park, Doyle, Goffman), to sooth the individual soul (Hughes, Goffman), to protect naked self-interest (Hughes)—a belief Goffman shared with his forerunners, which constrained his thinking. While Goffman was ready to take exception to other aspects of his professors' teaching, on this point he never dissented. The consequence of this belief for Goffman's work was profound. Like Doyle's work on racial etiquette, Goffman's theory of ceremony provides a weak challenge to the status quo. Goffman never entertained a belief in the view that freedom lies not behind social masks or fronts, and not through them in some creative way, but beyond them in some more fundamental human way.

Goffman's reluctance to take his research in this direction does not stop contemporary researchers from doing so. Future work in this Chicago tradition might profitably proceed by questioning the assumption of the necessity of fronts, recovering Spencer's insights into the relation between political power and etiquette, and extending Goffman's astute interactionist analysis of ceremony. The intellectual task ahead will be to link the politics of authenticity that Goffman repudiated with the tradition and tools that he advanced. By undertaking such a project, researchers will genuinely be in a position to move "beyond Goffman."

PART TWO

Simmel and Functionalist Sociology

INTRODUCTION

It was common wisdom for some years that functionalist sociology, starting with Talcott Parsons and continuing on through his students, had not engaged Simmel's sociology in a meaningful way. Parsons's important book, *The Structure of Social Action*, omitted a drafted chapter on Simmel, and with that decision the die was cast: Simmel was considered a second-rate thinker. The chapters in Part Two show the error of this version of sociological history. Parsons did omit the section on Simmel from the drafted chapter, and he did largely ignore him in his written publications; but Parsons and his students, Robert K. Merton and Kaspar D. Naegele, did draw on Simmel in their work in important ways. So did Lewis A. Coser, a student of Merton's and founder of "conflict functionalism." Through my interviews with Merton and Coser, and through my analysis of the unpublished writings and correspondence of Parsons and Naegele, the complex story of Simmel in functionalist thought emerged. It became clear to me that Simmel's writings had been fertile soil in which functionalist thought germinated.

Functionalism in sociology was not just a school of thought that achieved dominance in the middle years of this century. It was also a response to the times. As functionalist sociologists faced the national and world crises of their day—the Depression, World War II, Nazism, the Cold War—they drew on Simmel for inspiration, as well as for ammunition against their opponents. The following chapters explore these connections in detail. They ask questions about the role in Simmel's reception of such factors as intellectual resistance and rivalry, political ideology and critique. And they record the theoretical developments that accompany such extratheoretical factors. Here it seems appropriate to point out the larger significance of the data and interpretation in those essays.

Simmel's writings were pivotal to the problems of each thinker: to Parsons's struggle with the problem of social integration, to Naegele's attempt to comprehend the tragedy of genocide, to Merton's reconciliation of democracy and bureaucracy, and to Coser's battle with opponents of workers' rights. Each man found in Simmel not only intellectual inspiration, but moral wisdom. Simmel's concepts of form, of tragedy, of "visibility," and of conflict are more than intellectual tools; they are ethical principles. Each term reveals both the nature of social life and a direction for social action. It is this combination of fertile intellectual and moral imagination that makes a thinker a classic. The following chapters reveal that Simmel provided this needed combination to functionalist sociology during times of national social crisis. Rather than being peripheral to functional sociology, then, Simmel was a key architect of its intellectual and moral vision.

CHAPTER 3

SIMMEL'S CONTRIBUTION TO PARSONS'S ACTION THEORY AND ITS FATE

If the works of the Chicago School of sociology are often portrayed as models of engagé sociology, of social analysis close to pulse of social life, the writings of Talcott Parsons have usually been considered soulless, abstract, and arcane. But recent work on Parsons's life and writings (Buxton 1985; Vidich and Lyman 1985) reveal the error of this easy comparison. Parsons's sociological theory, including his reading of European social theory, has deep roots in his biography and particularly in his religious background and commitments.

Talcott Parsons was born into a Protestant household on 13 December 1902. Both of his parents followed the activist orientation of the Social Gospel movement. His mother, Mary A. Ingersol Parsons, was a suffragist and supporter of other progressive causes. His father, Edward S. Parsons, on graduating from Yale Divinity School, followed the social service orientation of the Social Gospel movement and became a home missionary. The elder Parsons's writings articulate the Social Gospel themes of social justice and Christian character. Writing in the preface to his *The Social Message of Jesus*, for example, Edward Parsons expressed the purpose of the work: to furnish the reader "with the disposition and motive which will make him of use in bringing in the kingdom" (Parsons 1912: 5). Talcott Parsons has noted that his own shift in career plans from biology and medicine to the social sciences was influenced by his father's example (Buxton 1985: 280; Martel 1979). In sociology Talcott Parsons would find a calling that afforded the opportunity to fulfill his Christian duty.

The collapse of the stock market and Great Depression made urgent this obligation. For the great world economic crisis was also a spiritual crisis, and sociology, the successor to theology, was poised to provide a secular resolution of the crisis. Parsons's early intellectual writings served this redemptive purpose: his systematic theory continued the theological mission of bringing about the Kingdom of God on Earth. To this end, his early writings focused on action from the point of view of its relation to ultimate values; he selected authors—Weber, Durkheim, Pareto, and Marshall—whose writings he believed analyzed action in terms of such values; he ultimately ignored authors—like Marx and Simmel—whose writings he believed excluded values from consideration; and he developed a theory of institutions which addressed ways of reuniting spirit and worldly conduct, a theory which would contribute to ending the spiritual malaise of America in the 1930s.

PARSONIAN PROBLEMATICS AND SIMMELIAN SOCIOLOGY

In the "Introduction to the Paperback Edition" of *The Structure of Social Action* (hereinafter referred to as *Structure*), Parsons included a now well-known and revealing note:

> Along with the American social psychologists notably Cooley, Mead, and W. I. Thomas, the most important single figure neglected in the *Structure of Social Action*, and to an important degree in my subsequent writings, is probably Simmel. It may be of interest that I actually drafted a chapter on Simmel for the *Structure of Social Action*, but partly for reasons of space finally decided not to include it. (Parsons 1968 [1937]: xiv)

This note is revealing for a number of reasons, but for the present purpose it points to two problems worthy of investigation: (1) What was the purpose of the section on Simmel, and (2) Why was it withdrawn from the published version of *Structure*?[1]

What was the purpose of the section on Simmel? A discussion of three issues or concerns that occupied Parsons's attention in the 1930s will provide some important background to that question.

1. Parsons's writings from the late 1920s to the late 1930s reveal a preoccupation with, on the one hand, the structure of individualistic capitalism, including an understanding that that structure alone was incapable of sustaining social order, and, on the other, an interest in identifying the cement that would hold society together. I call this preoccupation the *social cohesion problematic*. Parsons's search for the underlying causes of social cohesion is evident in his

teaching notes and other course materials from this period. Along with other positions, these courses considered Comte's "social instinct," Hobbes's "rational self-interest," and Rousseau's "common will" (Parsons 1929). These and many other views Parsons found inadequate based on what he reported to be a "vague realization" that they were "squeezing . . . the 'value' elements out of their interpretation of social life" (Parsons 1935b: 313). What accounts for this "vague realization?" If the earlier discussion of the influence of Parsons's Protestant background is accepted, an answer is immediately forthcoming: any focus on the causes of social cohesion that excluded moral values was incompatible with the calling of sociology conceived as a continuation of the Christian project of establishing the "Kingdom of God on Earth."

In his published writings Parsons's concern with the *social cohesion problematic* took the form of an "exhaustive critique" of the then current views, institutional economics and behaviorism in particular. The purpose of this critique was to determine the factors that were "responsible for their confident denials of the position I have taken up [i.e., on the importance of values in social life]" (Parsons 1935b: 313). As part of this review, Parsons examined the causal status of "formal sociology." This critique, however, is developed only in Parsons's unpublished writings. The issue is first mentioned in an unpublished review of Ferdinand Toennies' *Einfuehrung in die Soziologie*, where causal analysis is identified as "really a central difficulty for 'formal sociology'" (Parsons 1932b: 3). Only in the section on Simmel is this issue treated again in detail.

2. Related to the social cohesion problematic was another of Parsons's concerns in the 1930s, what I will call the *scope of sociology problematic*. This refers to Parsons's interest in delimiting the subject matter of sociology, specifically its "area of relatively autonomous causation" (Parsons 1930: 1). Given that the social sciences were considered by Parsons as a continuation of the Christian project, the importance of moral values would have to be admitted. Yet the social sciences were, in Parsons's view, all tangled together, and not one of them had focused explicitly on values. In addition, Parsons rejected those conceptions of the scope of sociology that resulted in sociology having no subject matter of its own. He rejected the "broad encyclopedic" view shared by Comte, Spencer, and Durkheim, an approach that made sociology a synthesis of all scientific knowledge. If such a view were followed, sociology "would have no principles peculiar to itself" (Parsons 1934: 529). He also rejected the "narrow encyclopedic" view held by Weber. This approach would make sociology the science of all social action and,

as such, leave undifferentiated the fields of politics, economics, and sociology. Only the "specific view" gave sociology "a subject matter essentially its own and not shared by any other systematic theoretical discipline" (p. 529). It was by following the specific view that Parsons arrived at a conception of sociology clearly demarcated from the other social sciences. Sociology would become "the science of the role of ultimate common ends . . . in human life" (p. 529). Parsons acknowledged that this position was not without precedent. As he stated in *Structure*:

> Simmel's [*Soziologie*] was, perhaps the first serious attempt to gain a basis for sociology as, in this sense, a special science. His formula is unacceptable for reasons that cannot be gone into here. But it was founded on sound insight, and the view just stated may be regarded as a restatement of its sound elements in more acceptable terms. (Parsons 1968 [1937]: 772–73)

This is no small role for Simmel in Parsons's paradigmatic grounding of sociology. Simmel was Parsons's exemplar for the solution of the *scope of sociology problematic*. While Parsons did not accept Simmel's specific formula for solving this problem, he did accept his general strategy. The reasons Parsons found Simmel's formula for the scope of sociology unacceptable are set out in the section on Simmel.

3. This brings us to the last issue Parsons was concerned with in connection with Simmel's writings. Parsons came to realize that the voluntaristic theory of action he was developing was, in certain respects, inherently limited. This limitation is characterized in an unpublished manuscript in the following way: it "is inherently limited in that it can deal only with a single individual at a time, seen in relation to his ends, the conditions of his actions and the norms regulating it" (Parsons 1935a: 18). Parsons's problem was to discover a way to move from the consideration of the action of a single individual to a consideration of "all the individuals in the community in relation to each other" (p. 18). Simmel's sociology was central to Parsons's solution to this problem, and this solution is a central part of the section on Simmel. It will be called in the following pages Simmel's *action theory contribution*.

In the foregoing discussion, I have identified three of Parsons's concerns and related them to Parsons's confrontation with Simmel's writings. These concerns were called the social cohesion problematic, the scope of sociology problematic, and the action theory contribution of Simmel's sociology. With these considerations as background, the purpose of the section on Simmel can now be addressed.

WHY DID PARSONS WRITE THE
UNPUBLISHED SECTION ON SIMMEL?

Parsons reveals the purpose of the section on Simmel on the first page of the drafted chapter:

> We are not ready to raise explicitly the question of the scope of sociology as such—that we have reserved for the final chapter. Here our concern is with the relation of Simmel's conception of social "form" to the conceptual schemas of our previous discussion. (Parsons 1936: 1)

This statement can be interpreted in terms of the three concerns previously identified. Simmel's relation to the scope of sociology problematic was not the central purpose of the section. The main issues that would be confronted in the section were the social cohesion problematic and the action theory contribution. Simmel's definition of the scope of sociology was but a "fruitful" starting point to arrive at the other two issues (p. 2).

Simmel arrives at his definition of sociology by distinguishing form from content. In this connection, content refers to the "different impulses, ends, interests" which motivate action. Social forms refer to the resultant modes of interaction. For Simmel, the proper domain of sociology would be an examination of the form of relationship only, the contents as such not being social. Sociology would leave to the other social sciences the investigation of the contents of social life apart from the forms of their realization. The field of politics, for example, would investigate political ends, drives, interests, and so on. Sociology would investigate the forms of social relationships in which these and other contents are realized, such as super- and subordination.

Parsons accepted Simmel's basic approach for defining the scope of sociology, that is, on the basis of analytical abstraction. Parsons was dissatisfied, however, with Simmel's specific formula for doing so. Parsons's basic dissatisfaction was best expressed in *Structure:*

> The main difficulty [with Simmel's definition of the scope of sociology] was that the view he took of the other social sciences precluded relating his concept of sociology to other analytical social sciences on the same methodological level. To him, sociology was the only abstract analytical science in the social field. (Parsons 1968 [1937]: 773)

Having stated his objections to Simmel's formula for the scope of sociology, Parsons was not inclined to thereby give up on Simmel entirely. Indeed, in the section on Simmel, Parsons is highly critical of those thinkers, like Theodore Abel (1929), who, having judged that Simmel's definition of the scope of sociology is wrong, concluded that the notion of form is therefore useless. This approach Parsons thought entirely mistaken:

> I also do not think it a useful procedure to define sociology as a "science of social forms." But that does not prevent recognizing that Simmel had very important insights into the facts and made a very genuine contribution . . . The critic, it seems to me, should first attempt to find out what it is, especially in relation to the empirical facts Simmel was concerned with. Then he should attempt to find out how the author arrived at the propositions the critic regards as objectionable. Only after having done this and having restated the author's empirical insights in more acceptable terms is he entitled to "criticize." The progress of science consists in the continual amendment and restatement of conceptual schemes, not in deciding they are "right" or "wrong." (Parsons 1936: 12)

These remarks are reproduced here because they state so clearly Parsons's rationale for the main purpose of the section on Simmel. In the section, Parsons attempts to arrive at a "restatement" of Simmel's notion of form "in more acceptable terms." I referred to this restatement earlier to as Simmel's action theory contribution. Before he arrived at that point, however, he would first have to show where Simmel went wrong. The manuscript proceeds with an examination of Simmel's concept of form in relation to the social cohesion problematic.

Parsons begins this discussion with a question: "What is meant when forms of relationship are spoken of as an independent variable, in the sense separable from content?" (p. 6). Can, for example, relationships of exchange, such as contractual relationships, be considered independent causes, or are they themselves the resultants of other factors? Parsons thought the latter, and reminds the reader that Durkheim had "shown conclusively" that relations of exchange such as contract rely on "noncontractual conditions" or normative rules that are ultimately based on moral values (p. 7). And "Simmel's conceptual scheme entirely fails to provide" (p. 8) moral values and norms.

In Parsons's view, Simmel's emphasis on forms of social relationships was an attempt to understand social life from the level of social structure. But "structure is . . . as such, not an explanatory category at all but a descriptive category" (p. 9). Therefore, "structure is something to be explained, not an explanation" (p. 12). Parsons was convinced that the "common ultimate value element" was "quite adequate for the explanation of the structural as well as any other aspect of social life" (p. 15). In Parsons's view, moral values, not social forms or structures, provided the source of social cohesion. Simmel's emphasis on forms, therefore, was incompatible with Parsons' solution to the social cohesion problematic. For this reason, it was unlikely that Simmel's sociology would play much of a role in Parsons's general theory.

While inadequate for explanatory purposes, Parsons believed that "form concepts are indispensable tools for sociological research" (p. 15). Parsons identified a twofold significance for the concept of social form. First was the attention it directed toward structure, "and above all [the] differentiation of structural types" (p. 15). Parsons would pursue this line of thinking in the next section of the chapter on Toennies's notions of *Gemeinschaft* and *Gesellschaft* (Parsons 1968 [1937]: 686–94). Second, the focus on forms of relationships provided an important corrective to his own action schema that tended to minimize the organic aspects of social relationships. "On the whole the action schema states social facts in a form which tends to minimize the structural elements. Hence the relationship schema, which throws them directly into the center of attention, is a *highly important descriptive corrective.*" Parsons adds: "*Simmel has performed a signal service in bringing these things so forcibly to our attention*" (Parsons 1936: 15–16; emphasis mine).

Given the tone and substance of the last statement, it is indeed surprising that the section on Simmel was omitted from the published version of *Structure*. In the next section, I examine the reasons for this turn of events. An appraisal of Donald N. Levine's approach to this question will serve to clarify our own view.

WHY DID PARSONS WITHDRAW THE SECTION ON SIMMEL?

Levine offers two explanations for Parsons's decision to withdraw the section on Simmel from *Structure*. The first is that at a certain point in Parsons's thinking he recognized that Simmel did not fit the convergence argument of *Structure*. Subsequent to this recognition, the section on Simmel was omitted from the published text (Levine 1985: 122–23). I will call this explanation the *nonconvergence argument*. The second explanation offered by Levine is that Simmel's definition of sociology as the *only* abstract analytical social science left economics in an ambiguous position. This ambiguity Parsons could not accept. "To commit himself totally to Simmel's framework would be to regard *economics* in a manner Parsons found unacceptable" (Levine 1985: 121). This I will call Levine's *ambiguity argument.* Both explanations are unacceptable for reasons that can now be explored.

The Nonconvergence Argument

Levine's nonconvergence argument is based on a reconstruction of what, on the face of it, appear to be plausible stages in Parsons's thinking about Simmel in relation to the convergence thesis of *Structure.* The first stage is represented by a passage from a footnote in Parsons's 1935 article "The Place of Ultimate Values in Sociological Theory":

> My own views have taken shape mainly in the course of a series of critical studies in European sociological theory. The important writers for my purposes may be divided into two groups—those starting from a positivistic and those from an idealistic background. I should maintain the thesis that the two groups have tended to converge on a conception somewhat like that which I shall outline in the present essay. Of the writers starting from a positivistic basis, two have been most important to me—Vilfredo Pareto and Emile Durkheim. Of the other group, the most important have been Max Weber, George [*sic*] Simmel, and Ferdinand Toennies. (Parsons 1935b: 283)

This is a striking passage, not only because it identifies that Simmel was "most important" to Parsons, but also because the German sociologist is included among those whom Parsons would argue in *Structure* had converged on a unified theory of action.

Levine then links two further stages: the final form of the convergence thesis (which occurred after Parsons had written the above note) and Parsons's decision to exclude the section on Simmel from *Structure.* "There can be no doubt that these two events were connected," Levine (1985: 123) concludes. In fact, Levine cites what he calls Parsons's "direct testimony" for this view:

> The decision not to include the Simmel chapter had various motives . . . The space problem was by no means the whole problem in relation to Simmel. *It is true that Simmel's program did not fit my convergence thesis.* (Levine 1985: 123, citing Parsons 1979: 1; emphasis Levine's)

It would appear that the nonconvergence argument is sound, especially given the above statement by Parsons. But, when closely examined, this explanation does not hold. Two problems can be identified.

First is the assumption central to Levine's nonconvergence argument, that Parsons had planned to consider Simmel in his convergence argument. Only with that assumption could Levine then argue that Parsons had changed his mind about Simmel when the convergence thesis was fully crystallized, and that this led Parsons to omit the section on Simmel. However, this argument fails to resolve two difficulties. One difficulty is that the footnote cited earlier includes Ferdinand Toennies as well as Simmel. Despite the fact that Toennies did not fit the convergence thesis of *Structure*, the section on Toennies from the drafted chapter was included in the published version. Even if Levine's nonconvergence argument were sound, then, it would not alone explain why Parsons decided to omit only the section on Simmel.

A second and more serious objection is that the nonconvergence argument is inconsistent with what Parsons in fact wrote about Simmel. That is, an examination of Parsons's writings and outlines for *Structure* indicate that Parsons had not changed his mind about Simmel. On the contrary, he had a very clear and consistent view of the relevance of Simmel's sociology to his theoretical pursuits. And this view had never been that Simmel had converged *on all essentials* with the views of the four writers analyzed in *Structure*. Parsons had an important, albeit limited, place for Simmel's "formal sociology" in his theory.

Consider once again the footnote from Parsons's 1935 essay on ultimate values. It states only that Simmel and the other writers mentioned "have tended to converge on a conception somewhat like that which I shall outline *in the present essay* (Parsons 1935b: 282; emphasis mine). Levine, however, does not reveal in what respects Simmel was relevant to the arguments Parsons presented therein. An examination of the essay will find that Parsons had one very clearly developed point to make regarding Simmel's relevance. Simmel is not mentioned by name, but it is clear that Parsons was referring to him:

> The "extensive" view of social life which looks upon it as a web of relationships between individuals may have something to teach us not revealed by the study of the action elements alone. (Parsons 1935b: 310)

What Parsons is referring to here is what was identified above as the action theory contribution of Simmel's sociology.

In addition, Parsons's working outlines for the proposed chapter on Simmel and Toennies do not reveal any intention of arguing that these two had converged with the others of the study. On the contrary, they reveal that Parsons considered their approaches as, in certain respects, complementary to his own. Consider, for example, the first extant outline of the contents of the chapter for *Structure*, the latter then having the title *Sociology and the Elements of Human Action*.

Chapter XVIII

Georg Simmel and Ferdinand Toennies formal sociology—its methodological status. Simmel's position and its difficulties. The formal approach to the theory of institutions. *Gemeinschaft* and *Gesellschaft* and the classification of institutions. Implications for the status of the means-ends schema. The scheme of social relationships as complement to that of action. Difficulties of the formal approach alone.

A later outline, which corresponds more closely to the contents of the drafted chapter, also emphasizes the links between the relationship schema and Parsons's action schema.[2] Note the more detailed title:

Georg Simmel and Ferdinand Toennies:
Social Relationships and the Elements of Action

Simmel and the methodology of formal sociology. The status of Structure. Difficulties of Simmel's position. Relation to institutions. *Gemeinschaft* and *Gesellschaft* and the classification of institutions. Gemeinschaft and "forms of expression." Descriptive importance of the relationship schema.

Finally, both the unpublished section on Simmel and the published version of *Structure*, minus that section, identify the descriptive importance of formal sociology as Simmel's central contribution to Parsons's action theory (cf. Parsons 1968 [1937]: 744–45, esp. 744, note 2).

It should be clear from the foregoing that Parsons held a relatively unvaried view of Simmel's sociology and its relationship to the theory of action he was developing. There is no indication that Parsons had changed his mind about Simmel from 1935 to 1937, when *Structure* was published. Moreover, there is no indication that Parsons ever considered the works of Simmel or Toennies as consistent with the convergence thesis of *Structure*. In all, none of these facts support Levine's nonconvergence argument.

What can be said, then, about the statement by Parsons considered by Levine to be a "direct testimony" for his nonconvergence argument? It would appear that Levine takes as a primary motive what is best considered, on balance, a proximate or secondary motive. Assessing the primacy of motives is, of course, a highly speculative procedure. But there are, at least, good reasons for this view. Central among these is that Parsons's statement was solicited. It was offered in response to a letter and other material sent by Jeffrey Alexander that broached the subject (Alexander 1979). Parsons's response was a three-page letter that expressed that he was "greatly interested" in the question of "the status of Simmel in my thinking," and remarked that he would attempt to "set the record straight" on the matter (Parsons 1979: 1). Given these remarks, it is curious that Parsons devotes only one sentence in this letter to Simmel's relation to his convergence thesis, the sentence Levine cites. It is difficult to conceive that in one sentence Parsons had "set the record straight" on a factor that was of central importance to his decision. Parsons does, however, offer considerably more lengthy discussions of two other unsolicited reasons for omitting the section on Simmel that do go a long way to setting the record straight. Levine does consider these two reasons offered by Parsons, but dismisses them for various reasons (Levine 1980 [1957]: xxvii–xxxi). Since these two reasons offered by Parsons are central to our own approach to this issue, a discussion of them, and Levine's grounds for dismissing them, will be deferred until the examination of Levine's argument is completed.

The Ambiguity Argument

Levine's *ambiguity argument* can best be summed up in his own words:

> To have published [the section on Simmel] in *Structure* or elsewhere, would have committed Parsons publicly to legitimating a direction for sociological theory that clearly "cut across" his own approach to theory building and would to some extent have been competitive with it. That would have required him to tolerate a degree of ambiguity that is enormously difficult for a highly motivated scientist to sustain. (Levine 1985: 124)

A close examination of Levine's reasoning will demonstrate that this conclusion is mistaken.

Levine argues that central among Parsons's interests following the completion of his dissertation was "establishing a sphere of
self-determination for his own fledgling discipline of sociology"
(Levine 1985: 119). At the same time, Parsons was no less determined to "guarantee the 'rights' of the field from which he had
migrated," that is, economics (Levine 1985: 121). Presumably, this is
because Parsons was socialized into that profession and "always
maintained the highest respect" for its achievements. Now in the
section on Simmel, Parsons registers his disagreement with Simmel's definition of the scope of sociology. Levine argues that Parsons
could not accept Simmel's program of "formal sociology." Not only
did it leave economics in a position that Parsons could not accept,
but also it was competitive with Parsons's own theoretical project
(Levine 1985: 124).

Thus far, there can be no disagreement with Levine's reasoning.
It is consistent with the above analysis of Parsons's scope of sociology problematic, and fits all the evidence of which we are aware.
The problem, however, is this: based on the reasoning sketched
above, Levine concludes that Parsons was led to omit the section on
Simmel from *Structure*. What evidence does Levine adduce to support his argument? At the outset it can be said that what little evidence is offered is misunderstood.

The central text that Levine cites for support is found in the
brief discussion of Simmel in the very last section of *Structure*, titled
"The Place of Sociology." The passage reads:

> The main difficulty for Simmel was that the view he took of
> the other social sciences precluded relating his concept of soci-
> ology to other analytical social sciences on the same method-
> ological level. To him sociology was the only abstract analyti-
> cal science in the social field. (Parsons 1968 [1937]: 773)

Note that this passage supports Levine's reasoning only up to the
point at which we are in full agreement, that is, prior to arguing
that this is the reason why the section on Simmel was withdrawn
from the published version of *Structure*. Considered in another way,
the passage only identifies *Simmel's* "main difficulty," not that this
difficulty implied anything about the status of the *section* on Simmel. In fact, there are good reasons for arguing that this passage has
no bearing at all on the question of Parsons's decision to omit the
section on Simmel.

First, the same passage appears in the version of *Structure*
before the decision to omit the section on Simmel was made (Par-

sons, PP, MSSA, Box 3). Second, the passage only identifies the "main difficulty" of Simmel's definition of the scope of sociology. But as was discussed earlier, this issue was not the central concern of the section on Simmel. Recall that on the first page of the draft Parsons wrote: "*We are not ready to raise explicitly the question of the scope of sociology as such—that we have reserved for the final chapter.* Here our concern is with the relation of Simmel's conception of social 'form' to the conceptual schemas of our previous discussion" (Parsons 1936: 1; emphasis mine). These lines explain why the passage Levine cites is found in the final chapter of *Structure* in the discussion of the "place of sociology." The relevance of that passage applies only to that discussion. The lines also reveal that the question of Simmel's definition of the scope of sociology is independent of the main questions that Parsons was concerned with in the section on Simmel. It follows that a problem in one area does not necessarily imply a problem in the other area.

The only other evidence Levine offers in support of his ambiguity argument is a passage from the section on Simmel: "In spite of the abstraction involved it [Simmel's form] is a mode of abstraction which directly *cuts across* the line of analysis into elements of action which has been our main concern" (Levine 1980 [1957]: liii, citing Parsons 1936: 9; emphasis Levine's). It is clear that this passage is central to Levine's understanding of this issue. The words "cuts across" are repeated in what can be considered the main statement of the ambiguity argument, which was cited above.

Levine interprets "cuts across" to mean that Simmel's definition of the scope of sociology was incompatible with Parsons's approach. Hence, Parsons made the decision not to publish the section on Simmel. This is a mistaken interpretation based, it seems, on Levine's reading of the section on Simmel only from the perspective of the scope of sociology problematic. What Parsons meant by these words is clearly revealed by examining the context of his remarks. For this reason it would be best to quote the argument in full:

> It is true that "*form* of relationship" is not a concrete descriptive category. Social relationship is the concrete entity. The "form" is not a "part" of this but an abstraction from it in a different direction. But it is not in *our* sense an analytical element. It is rather what may be tentatively called a "descriptive aspect." In spite of the abstraction involved it is a mode of abstraction which directly cuts across the line of analysis into elements of action which has been our main concern. (Parsons 1936: 9; emphasis in the original)

These remarks reveal that Parsons is not in this context interested in Simmel's abstraction of form *from content,* that is, the scope of sociology problematic. Rather, he is trying to arrive at some understanding of what kind of abstraction Simmel's "form" is *apart from content.* He eventually settles on calling it a "descriptive aspect." And, it is this descriptive approach of Simmel's that "cuts across" Parsons's own line of analysis into elements of action. In addition, while Parsons was convinced that this kind of conceptualization was not adequate as a sole approach to theory building, he exhibits no intolerance to "ambiguity," as Levine asserts. The importance of Simmel's descriptive approach in Parsons's thinking already established in these pages should be evidence enough of this view.

For these reasons we cannot accept Levine's analysis of the grounds for Parsons's decision to omit the section on Simmel from *Structure.* What, then, can be offered in its place? Shortly before his death Parsons "set the record straight" in his letter to Jeffrey Alexander. I see no reason to discount Parsons's own explanation of his decision, despite Levine's objections.[3] Parsons offers what can be considered two primary grounds for his decision. First is the problem of space:

> The decision not to include [the section on Simmel] had various motives. One of which was that as a very young and unknown author at the time I was submitting a manuscript which was already incredibly long and I might very well have jeopardized the chances of getting it published if it had been longer. (Parsons 1979: 1)

Parsons's concern with the length of his manuscript was not altogether unrealistic. He had earlier experienced considerable difficulty publishing a manuscript on Pareto, in part, because of its length (Parsons 1932a). But this problem cannot be the whole story. The section on Toennies was included in *Structure,* but set in smaller type. Why didn't Parsons do the same for the section on Simmel? To answer this question Parsons reveals another kind of concern that singles out Simmel as problematic on quite different grounds:

> [Simmel's] position had been used as relatively few people are still aware as the takeoff point for *an attempt to build social system theory which I considered to be fundamentally mistaken.* This began in Germany with a large work by Leopold von Wiese, with the title, *Beziehungslehre.* This had appeared somewhere near the time I was a student in Heidelberg . . . It

had a certain vogue there but the theme was taken up by the late Howard Becker . . . Becker built it into a large book which was an adaptation of the Wiese position and went under the title *Wiese-Becker*. Indeed, for a few years Becker and I were rivals for the leadership of the introduction of German Sociology into this country. If I played down Simmel, certainly Becker even more drastically played down Weber. (Parsons 1979: 1-2; emphasis mine)

Parsons's rivalrous concern with competitive advantage was not unreasonable. Others have pointed out the similar points of departure and other parallels of Parsons's and Wiese's social systems theories (cf. Konig 1968; Liebersohn 1982). For example, both had been critical of Herbert Spencer and attempted to lay the groundwork of a voluntaristic sociology. If there was an approach to theory that directly "cut across" and was competitive with Parsons's approach it was surely the *Systematic Sociology* of Wiese-Becker (cf. Paharik 1983: Ch. 4). In addition, Parsons found an immediate competitor in Becker, who briefly joined the Harvard sociology department as lecturer in the fall of 1935, and was recommended the following year by the same department for a three-year appointment as assistant professor. While the administration did not approve Becker's recommendation, the problem of theoretical competition between Parsons and Becker continued.[4]

I submit that Parsons was able to resolve both the problem of space and the problem of theoretical competition. This resolution was not accomplished, however, by withdrawing the *entire* section on Simmel from *Structure*. As I have indicated, a discussion of the descriptive aspect of Simmel's "relationship schema," which Parsons identified in the draft as an important corrective to his "action schema," was included in *Structure* (pp. 744–45 ff.). Rather, the two problems were resolved by omitting the lengthy critical discussion of Simmel's "form," including the discussion of Wiese, and accommodating Simmel's more positive contribution in a separate section of the study. Not only does this explanation follow closely Parsons's own account of his decision, but it also fits all the facts available to us.

CONCLUSION

This chapter has examined the fate of Georg Simmel in Parsons's early writings, especially *The Structure of Social Action*. This book would provide the grounding of American functionalist sociology. Simmel was found to occupy a rather limited place in this theory. On the one hand, Simmel's substantive writings lacked the emphasis on moral values and norms Parsons considered essential to his sociology conceived as a continuation of the Christian project. On the other hand, certain aspects of Simmel's methodology Parsons found central to the initial stages of that project. Limited thus to methodological significance, Simmel would not play an important role in Parsons's later writings. Some of Parsons's students would find this limitation unacceptable, and attempt to incorporate other aspects of Simmel's sociology into the functionalist paradigm.

CHAPTER 4

A NOTE ON KASPAR D. NAEGELE

Kaspar D. Naegele (1923–1965) occupies a distinctive place in
the American Simmel reception. He was not only a native German
whose academic training fell within the intellectual horizon of Georg
Simmel; he was also a neighbor and family friend of the Simmels' in
Germany.[1] In addition, Naegele lectured regularly on the classical
sociologist, planned to write his intellectual biography, and actively
promoted the American Simmel reception. He was a recognized
Simmel scholar whose own writings have a distinctly Simmelian
style. Yet, ironically, Naegele's efforts to Americanize Simmel
appear to have been largely ignored. The absence of Naegele's work
from the important review, "Simmel's Influence on American Sociology" (Levine et al. 1976), at once symbolizes and helps to constitute this curious fate.

Perhaps this neglect can be understood, without being justified,
as a result of nationalistic bias. While he earned his Ph.D. from Harvard University in 1952 and published widely in American sociological journals, Naegele was a Canadian citizen and spent most of his
academic career at the University of British Columbia (P. Naegele
1970; Mills and Jones 1965; Jamieson 1965). Or, perhaps the neglect is
attributable to the fact that he founded no school of thought or special
theory-branch. While Naegele has many admirers, he left few, if any,
disciples.[2] But more important, Naegele's efforts to incorporate Simmel's thought into Parsonian theory were repeatedly frustrated.
Despite Parsons's admiration for Naegele and his contributions to
sociology, he and his system of thought resisted Simmelian inroads.

SIMMEL'S TRAGIC VIEW OF LIFE AND PARSONIAN THEORY

Naegele was openly dissatisfied with the limited appreciation
for Simmel's work in mid-century America. An early paper—from

Naegele's first year as a student in the Parsons-led Department of Social Relations at Harvard—best expresses this discontent (Naegele 1948). Acknowledging Parsons's own critique of Simmel, Naegele wrote, "Admittedly [Simmel's] logic concerning form and content in relation to social process admits of easy refutation. His definition of sociology is probably untenable. Yet Simmel is more than that . . . it is Simmel as *lebensphilosoph* that social sciences might well reevaluate." Naegele identified two aspects of Simmel's work for American sociologists to consider. The first is Simmel's tragic view of life, particularly as expressed in *Lebensanschauung* (Simmel 1922); the second is Simmel's heuristic importance, his subtle and various insights into everyday life that "provide fertile leads." Characterizing Simmel as a "social-psychologist," Naegele conceded that while "one might readily criticize [him] on methodological grounds, [he] invariably points out the subtleties attached to daily occurrences." In sum, Simmel "evolved a highly suggestive sociology of everyday life and gave it the framework of a tragic view of life" (Naegele 1948: 16).

Naegele recognized that these two aspects of Simmel's sociology were not particularly congenial to the thoughtways of American sociologists. He maintained, however, that together they were a necessary corrective: "Perhaps Simmel is too European and pushes subtlety too far in all directions; for American sociology, however, this is a necessary emphasis" (Naegele 1948: 16–17). Much of the contemporary social science literature Naegele found "external" and "flat." A receptivity to Simmel's work, he argued, would help restore an appreciation of the "full bloodedness of society" (Naegele 1948: 18).

Naegele's insistence on intellectual subtlety over crassness; his appreciation of the "full bloodedness of society" and displeasure in concepts devoid of the pulse of life; and his insight into the centrality of the tragic and paradoxical in life—all symbolically manifest his peculiar life circumstances. As a European with a classical German Gymnasium education, his confrontation with what others have called the "intellectual mediocrity" of American social science in the 1940s and 1950s (Levine et al. 1976: 1129) must have been cause for perturbation. Moreover, he was a witness to and victim of wartime inhumanity (see P. Naegele 1970), a German émigré who narrowly escaped Hitler's "final solution." These circumstances alone account for Naegele's penchant for the tragic. Like Simmel, he thought life was bedeviled by a metaphysical paradox: "that in order to live we must produce the very things that destroy us. That is our tragedy" (Naegele 1948: 16).

Naegele's writings express a hope that American sociology would be open to Simmel's tragic metaphysics of life. Despite repeated attempts to link the work of Parsons and Simmel, he was unable to see this hope fulfilled. In part, this failure was due to an incompatibility between the basic metaphysical premises of the two sysytems. As identified by Bershady (1973: Ch. 5), Parsons's metaphysical premises are best considered a variant of Whitehead's organicism. Reality is an organic whole tending toward equilibrium. Strains and tensions coming both from within and without any part of the whole disrupt the organized totality. Despite the inevitability of such critical disruptions, they cannot be considered tragic. This is because they do not arise from the very nature of reality, the telos of which is toward equilibrium. Simmel's metaphysics, by contrast, is a characteristically tragic one because the destructive forces of life "spring forth from the deepest levels" of life itself (Simmel 1968: 43; see also, Weingartner 1962: 83).

But the difficulties of linking Parsonian and Simmelian thought were not only a result of theoretical incompatibility; they were also a result of Parsons's own resistance to incorporate Simmel's and Naegele's tragic views of life. Evidence of his opposition can be found in the Simmel selections of *Theories of Society* (Parsons et al. 1961). As Table 3 shows, an early list of contents for the anthology of readings, collected by Shils and Parsons, included two Simmel selections. Parsons sent Naegele a copy of that outline and asked him

TABLE 3 Three Versions of Simmel Selections for *Theories of Society*

Early List of Contents[a]	*Kaspar Naegele's Suggestions*[b]	*Final Selections*[c]
"Determination of Social Relations by Numbers"	"Sociability" (to replace first selection in early list)	"The Sociology of Sociability"
"On rationality" (from *Philosophie des Geldes*, no page numbers specified)	"Super- and Subordination"	"On Superordination and Subordination"
	"Conflict and Tragedy of Culture"	"Secrecy and Group Communication"
		"On Conflict"
		"Faithfulness and Gratitude"

[a] (Shils and Parsons, n.d.)
[b] (Naegele 1954)
[c] (Parsons, et al. 1961)

for his comments (Parsons 1954). Naegele's response identified several additional selections, including Simmel's essays on the conflict and tragedy of culture (Simmel 1968). The essay on the tragedy of culture, however, was not included in the final list of selections. This attempt to introduce tragic metaphysical premises into Parsonian functionalism was ultimately, perhaps inevitably, unsuccessful. Both Parsonian theory and Parsons himself were not open to Simmel's thought at that level.[3]

This resistance to Naegele's preferred metaphysical premises was offset by what he perceived as an openness by other functionalists to his basic methodological premise: the best way to comprehend and order the paradoxes of life was through the development and use of paradoxical expressions. Naegele called this approach a "bedeviled perspective":

> For if the patterns we discover in nature or in man are often paradoxical, how can we do justice to them—be it in the act of comprehension or in an attempt to convey our shifting comprehension—unless we ourselves . . . are similarly bedeviled, similarly full of an incongruity that never adds up, but always makes sense?" (Naegele 1956: 179)

Naegele sought to develop a "paradoxical point of view in social science" and thought "the works of Simmel [were] probably the best single source" for developing that perspective (Naegele 1949a: 15, note 8). While he never provided a systematic analysis of the basis or function of paradox in Simmel's social thought, he did twice offer sustained discussion of the matter. One is in the essay, "Attachment and Alienation: Complementary Aspects of the Work of Durkheim and Simmel (Naegele 1958), his contribution to the Durkheim-Simmel commemorative issue of the *American Journal of Sociology*. A list of the key points of that article as they pertain to the device of paradox will serve to clarify Naegele's views:

1. As compared with Durkheim, whose writings develop and grow out of each other, Simmel's writings are connected but uncumulative. Simmel uses a constant "formula" to analyze a variety of phenomena.
2. That "formula" is variously called the "paradoxical use of terms"; the "juxtaposition of opposites"; or the use of "reciprocal distinctions" or "complementary notions."
3. Simmel's paradoxical use of terms is an essential characteristic of his thought.

4. The main function of reciprocal distinctions is to clarify the structure of the social. Simmel's sociology is not explanatory. It represents reality so that, eventually, its structure can be explained.
5. The main problem of Simmel's reciprocal distinctions is that they were developed in an ad hoc fashion. This leaves the researcher in a quandary. By what criteria does one choose which set of distinctions to explain?
6. The main task of sociology with regard to Simmel's distinctions is to translate them into the language of empirical research.
7. The main limitation of Simmel's paradoxical use of terms is that it involves "style rather than method" and "cannot be directly continued."

The other sustained discussion of paradox is found in a memorandum he prepared for the Harvard University project on the "Comparative Study of Values" (Naegele 1949b; see also Kluckhohn et al. 1951). This essay examined the social science literature on American culture and found in it "a marked tendency to 'discover' in America a series of paradoxes and conflicts" (Naegele 1949b: 50). It singled out for special attention the work of Robert Lynd (1946), his former teacher at Columbia University. Lynd's characterization of American culture as an assemblage of contradictory assumptions and contrasting rules of the game is just one example of this tendency. Naegele's memorandum reveals that Lynd shared this procedure with others, including Simmel, Tocqueville, and Weber. In this manuscript, Naegele's attempt to legitimize Simmel's paradoxical use of terms took the form of a search for an intellectual tradition. By locating a tradition of paradox in the sociological literature, a tradition in common with the intellectual foundations of functionalism, the way was being cleared for a greater receptiveness to Simmel.

But defining a tradition and having others accept and work within that tradition are two different matters. Ten years after the memorandum, Bendix and Berger (1959) rediscovered virtually the same intellectual tradition and presented a methodological strategy—paired concepts and the perspective of "dual tendencies"—remarkably similar to Naegele's. They appeared skeptical, however, about the possibilities for acceptance of their approach, noting that it "can be exemplified from the work of sociologists but on the whole it runs counter to major trends in the field" (Bendix 1970: 121). The authors clearly imply that Parsonian functionalism was a most important opposing major trend. Still later, Levine, et al. (1976) singled out Simmel's dualisms as a neglected area of sociological research.

As Merton (1973) and others have argued, rediscoveries such as these are symptomatic of resistance to ideas. The ongoing rediscovery of Simmel's analysis of dual tendencies—by Naegele in 1949, Bendix-Berger in 1959, and Levine et al. in 1976—suggests resistance that goes to the very core of sociological thought. The difficulties Naegele faced when attempting to incorporate Simmel into Parsonian thought, then, were just one instance of this more general resistance.

"Severalness" and the Social Order

Naegele's goal of incorporating Simmel's paradoxical use of concepts into functionalism was salvaged and creatively reintroduced at the methodological level through the term "severalness." It is a difficult term and notion to comprehend or characterize. Daniel Bell commented on a drafted paper by Naegele written when both were Fellows at the Center for Advanced Study in the Behavioral Sciences at Stanford. He called it a "curious term" because it had "both a poetic quality and a 'German' metaphysical quality (like dasein)." In addition, he found the "state of being" thought that was suggested by the suffix "ness" made the term "elusive" (Bell 1958: 1).

What Bell meant by saying the term had a "poetic" quality is not clear, nor is it clear what the implications for social research would be if it had such qualities, whatever they may be. Moreover, the "state of being" thought conveyed by the suffix "ness," far from making the term elusive, actually provides the key to making some sense of the notion. It suggests that severalness is not a heuristic concept, a fiction designed merely to aid in the comprehension of reality. Nor is it an analytical concept, in the Parsonian sense. Rather the term reveals its origins in Naegele's metaphysical and methodological premises, revealed earlier. That is, the notion is based on Naegele's commitment to a paradoxical-tragic view of reality and a realist epistemology tempered, perhaps, by Parsons's Whiteheadian warnings about the "fallacy of misplaced concreteness." 'Severalness' appears to have been fashioned to convey what Naegele believed was a complex paradoxicality of life and thought, a view he believed he shared with Simmel. Stated in Naegelean terms, severalness is the single term that captures the indefinite number of ways in which an incongruous reality, while never adding up, nevertheless makes sense. At the risk of obscuring more than clarifying, it could be said that there is no severalness, only kinds of severalness.

Consider the variety of senses of severalness found in one article of Naegele's (1957) on the social context of communication in a hospital. Among the usages he discussed (1) severalness of purpose: organizations pursuing several, opposing aims at once (e.g., teaching hospitals); (2) methodological severalness: the necessity of several perspectives brought to bear when thinking about an organization (i.e., the perspectives of each of the social sciences); (3) process severalness: society goes in several directions at once (i.e., circles, back and forth); and (4) interactional severalness: a severalness to human exchanges (e.g., formal and informal). By employing this term in his own work, Naegele sought to bring Simmel's paradoxical perspective into functionalist thought. This effort is most clearly manifest in Naegele's role as an articulator of Parsonian functionalist thought.

According to Elaine Cumming, a close friend and sometimes-editor of Naegele's writings (e.g., Naegele 1970), Naegele was one of Parsons's brightest students; he grasped the latter's theoretical system quickly and completely, and he had the capacity to translate Parsons's cumbersome conceptual framework into more easily understood nontechnical prose.[4] Available commentary on his teaching abilities testifies as well to his ability to render Parsons intelligible in face-to-face discussions (Mills and Jones 1965; Jamieson 1965). Parsons must have recognized the value of having an able articulator of his theory. After taking his Ph.D., Naegele spent the 1953–1954 academic year on a Rockefeller grant as visiting professor at the Institute for Sociology of the University of Oslo, Norway. Naegele described the purpose of his visit in these words:

> I am to give a series of lectures and seminars and help with various pieces of research (mostly theses). One of my tasks is to represent various aspects of Parsons' ever-growing work and show, to the best of my abilities, the bearing this does or could have on past and present empirical research. (Naegele 1953: 1)

Also, it was during this time at Oslo that Naegele corresponded with Parsons about the contents of *Theories of Society*, the anthology of social theory of which Naegele was to become a contributor and joint editor.

Naegele's role as articulator or interpreter of Parsons's functionalist language was renewed during this joint editorship. Naegele (1961) wrote the opening essay of the two-volume work, "Some Observations on the Scope of Sociological Analysis." This essay prepared the reader in nontechnical language for what Parsons would do more technically in his following essay (Parsons et al. 1961: 30–79).

The notion of severalness figures prominently in Naegele's essay generally as well as in the performance of this more specific task, as is illustrated in this important passage from the essay:

> Good sociology is inevitably haunted by the labyrinthine immensity of human affairs; it is also always within reach of a governing assumption . . . that this immensity exhibits intelligible and communicable regularities and that these, at least for the time being, are of several kinds. (Naegele 1961: 5)

Much of the chapter is devoted to identifying and discussing the kinds of severalness that accompany the study of society. Many of these are of Simmelian provenance. For example, one of sociology's concerns is with what Naegele called the "severalness of efforts" (Naegele 1961: 7), or, the simultaneous involvement in a web of multiple groups (Simmel 1955). Another concern is "the severalness of what we have comprehended and what we have yet to unravel" (Naegele 1961: 5–6) about other people, or the combinations of knowledge and ignorance that make possible human relationships (Simmel 1950: 307–76). But other forms of severalness represent Parsonian concerns and concepts. The "several elements" (Naegele 1961: 8) of concrete social arrangements, for example, referred to Parsons's classification of structural components, that is, roles, collectivities, norms and values (Parsons et al. 1961). The "*several* comprehensible realms" (Naegele 1961: 10) that order and accompany events in the world characterized Parsons's "four-system paradigm," that is, culture, social system, personality, and behavioral organism (Parsons 1951).

The notion severalness has not stood the test of time. It has no concrete referent and was employed by Naegele mainly as a metaphor for multiplicity. But the difficulties he encountered in synthesizing Simmel and Parsons must not obscure the lasting value of his message. Naegele was one of the first American sociologists to champion Simmel's contributions to the sociology of everyday life; and he was a ceaseless advocate of Simmel's tragic view of life, paradoxical formulations, and intellectual subtlety. The sociologists of everyday life who followed him, as well as the contemporary symbolic interactionists, inherited his mantle, and the spirit of his work lives on in theirs.

CHAPTER 5

ROBERT K. MERTON'S EXTENSION OF SIMMEL'S *ÜBERSEHBAR*

It has been over two decades since the publication of the important study, "Simmel's Influence on American Sociology" (Levine et
al. 1976). In the intervening years, the project of understanding the
reception of Georg Simmel's thought by American sociologists has
not progressed very far. Little has been accomplished beyond clarifi-
cation of the role Simmel's writings played in the early work of Talcott Parsons (see chapter 3). In contrast, studies of Simmel's place in
and influence on European social thought continue unabated
(Gephardt 1982; Jaworski 1983; Levine 1985; Frisby 1986; Liebersohn 1988; Levine 1989). The chapters in this section of the book
seek to contribute to correcting this imbalance by examining Simmel's reception by American functionalist sociologists in the middle
part of this century. Here I report on one result of the larger research
project: an analysis of Robert K. Merton's extension of Simmel's
term "*Übersehbar*," or "surveyable."[1]

While Merton was familiar with Simmel's writings since at
least his years at Harvard (Merton 1980: 69), he did not draw on
Simmel's work in a sustained way until the mid-1950s. It was an
opportune time to revisit Simmel. Kurt H. Wolff had recently completed his English translation of selections from Simmel's *Soziologie*
(Simmel 1950). Other translations of Simmel's work were forthcoming (Simmel 1955; 1959). Also, under Merton's direction, Lewis
A. Coser had completed his dissertation, "Toward a Sociology of
Social Conflict" (Coser 1954), which was, in part, subsequently published (Coser 1956a). In sum, by the time of Merton's revisit, Simmel
was becoming respectable intellectual property. Of course, Merton's
own use of Simmel would contribute substantially to Simmel's
growing reputation in the sociological community.

Merton has revealed that the purpose of his mid-1950s reexamination of Simmel's *Soziologie* was to assist his own thinking on a number of problems he was working on at the time. That is, the text was used to stimulate his own thought. The vehicle for that stimulation was a series of two year-long seminars (1955–1956; 1956–1957) on "Selected Problems in the Theory of Organizations."[2] An outcome of those seminars and Merton's reexamination of Simmel was the 106-page chapter, "Continuities in the Theory of Reference Groups and Social Structure," published in the second, enlarged edition of *Social Theory and Social Structure* (Merton 1957). This chapter contains Merton's main contribution to the American Simmel reception, a contribution with theoretical and practical consequences.

Merton, Simmel, and the Problem of Democracy in Post-War America

One of the problems on which the attention of Merton and his students was focused during his seminars on Simmel's *Soziologie* was the reconciliation of bureaucracy and democracy, an issue that was part of a much larger dialogue on freedom and control in America after World War II (Berger et al. 1954). The necessity of a reconciliation became apparent to scholars of the period for at least three reasons. First, and most obviously, the events of history suggested the connection between the wartime atrocities and bureaucratic structure and personality. George Orwell's *Nineteen Eighty-four* (1949) provided a literary reminder of similar prospects in a democracy. Second, the pessimism of past thought on bureaucracy, most notably Weber's "iron cage" imagery and Michels' "iron law of oligarchy," was incompatible with the optimism after World War II (cf. Gouldner 1955). From such optimism flowed the sense of possibility of a reconciliation. And third, empirical research into bureaucracy had revealed that the informal structure of the workers differed considerably from the formal structure instituted by management. Reflection on this research gave rise to questions on the role of democracy in industrial relations (e.g., Bendix 1947: 502).

Two of Merton's students attempted unsuccessfully to reconcile democratic values with bureaucratic structure. Peter Blau (1956) based his efforts on the distinction between the determination and the implementation of social goals. He argued that while the determination of goals requires democratic means, such as majority decision, the implementation of goals requires bureaucratic means, such as efficiency. So long as these two purposes and the appropriate means to achieve them are kept distinct, "bureaucracies [do] not violate democratic values" (Blau 1956: 107). However, this distinction did not lead to much of a reconciliation at all, as Blau himself acknowledges; for major corporations and political parties are in a position to both determine goals and implement them. In such pervasive and powerful organizations, then, "democratic processes are in particular danger of being undermined by bureaucratization" (Blau 1956: 108).

Alvin Gouldner (1954) also attempted to reconcile bureaucracy and democracy. Like Blau, Gouldner begins by creating distinctions. Three patterns of industrial bureaucracy are identified and analyzed. One of these patterns, the "representative," was shown to be consistent with democratic principles. The alternative to representative bureaucracy, what Gouldner called "punishment-centered bureaucracy," was closer to despotism than to democracy. Unlike Blau, however, Gouldner does not attempt a reconciliation of bureaucracy and democracy on a theoretical plane. This is because, in Gouldner's view, a reconciliation can occur only at the level of practice. Gouldner (1954: 245) portrays his study as the report of a "social clinician" who has analyzed the ills and identified the options available for a healthy body-social. He offers his study to the "policy makers" as evidence that a reconciliation was possible. In this way he had hoped to contribute to the advance of "democratic potentialities" in a bureaucratic society. Yet, as Michael Burawoy (1982) has convincingly argued, Gouldner did not sufficiently fulfill this task. By abstracting "representative bureaucracy" from the type of economic system in which it was embedded, Gouldner misperceived the conditions of its possibility. Gouldner ended up, in Burawoy's (1982: 836) words, "celebrating potentialities" rather than accurately assessing the possible.

In contrast to these attempts, Merton's intellectual response to the problem of bureaucracy and democracy was to create an image of the structure and process of bureaucracy as inherently democratic. There can be no irreconcilable differences between the two for, by its very nature, bureaucracy is democratic. To be more specific, democratic principles are inherent in bureaucratic systems in three forms: (1) the authority of those who rule comes from below; (2) the needs of the individual and the needs of the system operate through a mechanism of checks and balances; and (3) the autonomy of the individual is guaranteed by the system. Merton's development of Simmel's ideas on visibility, or *Übersehbar*, are integral to his resolution of this issue.

The term *Übersehbar* is not a fully developed term in Simmel's social theory. According to Merton, it is a "tacit concept" which Merton sought to develop systematically, that is, in a manner uncongenial to Simmel's style of thinking.[3] The key text to which Merton refers in this connection is the following passage from Simmel's discussion of aristocracies in *Soziologie*:

> There also is an *absolute* limit beyond which the aristocratic form of the group can no longer be maintained. The point at which it breaks down is determined in part by external, in part by psychological circumstances. If it is to be effective as a whole, the aristocratic group must be "surveyable" by every single member of it. Each element must be personally acquainted with every other. (Simmel 1950: 90)

This passage served as Merton's "point of departure" (Merton 1957: 310, note 46) for developing the structural property of groups he called "visibility or observability" and which he defined as "the extent to which the norms and the role-performances within the group are readily open to observation by others" (Merton 1957: 319). Since about a quarter of the "Continuities" chapter is devoted to an analysis of the group property, a complete discussion of Merton's ideas cannot be carried out in these pages. However, some comments on Merton's use of Simmel's term are in order.

First, one might question, along with Robert Bierstedt (1981: 481, note 89), the wisdom of Merton's translation of Simmel's term *Übersehbar* as "visible" or "observable." As represented in the above quotation, Kurt H. Wolff's translation of this imprecise and complex term was "surveyable." Merton's justification for changing the translation was that the "sense of the original seems somewhat better approximated . . . by the words 'visible' or 'observable,' with the connotation of being visible at a glance, of being readily observable" (Merton 1957: 320, note 58). But the sense of the original is a function not only of what the author has written but also of what the reader brings to the text. In this regard it might be instructive to point out that Merton's apparent models for this term relate to situations of copresence. These models are friendship and the difference between being under someone's tutelage and being independent.[4] Simmel's use of *Übersehbar* in the passage quoted above includes the connotation of face-to-face contact, but is not limited to it. Moreover, other references to the concept in Simmel's *Soziologie* do not at all imply being "visible at a glance" (e.g., Simmel 1950: 102, 110). In addition, as Bierstedt argues (1981: 481, note 89), Merton's use of 'visible' as translation for *Übersehbar* opens up a messy can of metaphysical worms. Merton includes both norms and role-performances among those "things" that are more or less visible. But norms are not physical objects. And in what sense norms can be "seen" is not clarified by Merton.

Second, Merton uses two words, visible *or* observable, to refer to one group property. However, his discussion of the property reveals that the terms are used in two different ways, and used inconsistently to refer to those two ways. On the one hand, the terms refer to a *property of an observable*, that is, the extent to which some behavior pattern is obvious or hidden to others in a group. An office romance, employee pilferage, or worker productivity, for example, are all more or less open for others to see. On the other hand, the terms are also used by Merton to refer to an *attribute of a social position*. This sense is revealed in the following passage:

> "Visibility," then, is a name for the extent to which the structure of a social organization provides occasion to those variously located in that structure to perceive the norms obtaining in the organization and the character of role-performance by those manning the organization. (Merton 1957: 350)

As an illustration of this meaning, and to continue with the above examples, some positions in an organization or group are structured such that they allow the incumbent the opportunity to be well-informed about office romances, employee pilferage, and so forth. Other positions are structured in such a way that awareness of such matters is limited.[5]

Finally, it is not altogether clear which of the two senses referred to above, if either, can be considered a conceptual refinement of Simmel's term *Übersehbar*. For example, Merton's structural rendering of the term misses the phenomenological penumbra surrounding the term: To what extent and in what ways may one's personal acquaintance with others be determined or scrutinized? That Merton's rendering of the term bears no precise relation to Simmel's original is highlighted by Lewis Coser's reference in this connection to the "marvelous alchemy" through which Simmel's "incidental remarks" were turned by Merton into functionalist analysis (Coser 1975: 97). If Coser meant what he wrote, then not only is he implying that Merton turned something base into something better; he is also implying that the methods used to make this change were less than purely scientific.

While it can be argued that the specifics of Merton's extension of Simmel's *Übersehbar* bear little resemblance to the original, the general problem each was pursuing was similar: What are the conditions under which societal structures persist or dissolve? Simmel was concerned, in that section of *Soziologie* where Merton discovered his term *Übersehbar*, with the "vital conditions of an aristocracy" (Simmel 1950: 91). Merton was interested in the vital conditions of democracy. Under what conditions do social systems dissolve and under what conditions do they persist or thrive? According to Merton's reading of Simmel, the latter had proposed that aristocracies dissolve when they become so large that each member is no longer visible to the other. Taking his cue from Simmel, Merton identified a similar problem in democracies. What leads to the social dissolution of democracies is not distance within the elite strata, but distance between the leaders and the led.

Whether they are bureaucrats or politicians, authority figures need to be aware of the norms and conduct of those they govern. This is because the legitimacy of their orders is granted or conferred by the governed, and only if those orders conform to the norms of the group. On the one hand, those directives that depart considerably from the norms of the governed are not likely to be followed, "or followed only under duress, with the result that the once legitimate authority becomes progressively converted into the exercise of 'naked power.'" On the other hand, when orders are contained within the limits of the group norms of the governed, "authority remains more or less intact" (Merton 1957: 340). For Merton, it follows that "visibility of both norms and role-performances is required if the structure of authority is to operate effectively." In other words, visibility of this kind constitutes a "functional requirement" (Merton 1957: 340, 341) of effective and stable authority.

If visibility is required to avoid authority reverting to naked power, then access to the behavior of the governed must have limits lest it lead to a Hobbesian state of nature. Merton recognized the dangers of intrusions on privacy when he wrote, "Full visibility of conduct and unrestrained enforcement of the letter of normative standards would convert a society into a jungle" (Merton 1957: 345). Consequently, the countervailing functional requisite of "limits upon full visibility" is necessary if society is not to result in a Hobbesian battleground.

Merton devotes a good deal of space to developing the details of the argument, which I have presented only in its boldest outlines. These details have only a superficial relation to Simmelian ideas. However, Simmel's general analysis of the vital conditions of social systems helped Merton resolve the problem of reconciling bureaucracy and democracy. The result was a justification of both authoritative control and individual autonomy as countervailing system requirements. Moreover, with the concept of a "functionally optimum degree of visibility" (Merton 1957: 344), the variability of control or autonomy throughout existing organizations or societies can be accounted for and justified as being functionally necessary.

THE EMBLEMATIC FUNCTION OF SIMMELIAN ANALYSIS

Further insight into Merton's extension of Simmel's *Übersehbar* can be gleaned by drawing a comparison with the fate of Durkheim's anomie in functionalist sociology. Besnard's (1986; 1987; 1988) studies of "the strange career of anomie" are especially helpful in this connection. After charting the many, various, and confusing meanings of Durkheim's term in sociological literature, Besnard attributes this history, in part, to the "relative obscurity" of the term in Durkheim's work itself; but, he also focuses on the term's misappropriation by American functionalists. He argues, for example, that Merton developed the term (e.g., Merton 1957: 131–60) in a way that differed considerably from Durkheim's usage. Despite the term's subsequent irregular and inconsistent uses, however, it became something of a success. What explains this strange fate of anomie?

Besnard suggests that anomie was a success because it served as "a kind of emblem of normal research practice" (Besnard 1988: 94). Those participating in anomie research at the height of the term's success in the 1960s were engaged in a repeat of the 1930s Big East revolt against the Chicago School of sociology. They were, in effect, displaying their allegiance to the research approach of structural functionalism in opposition to the "research practices which the Chicago School had developed: ecological analysis and fieldwork" (Besnard 1988: 94). Functionalist research was characterized by reference to the classics, which provided hypotheses, and the use of positivistic research techniques, which provided the means to test those hypotheses. "Thanks to *anomie*," Besnard writes, "sociologists had at their disposal classic authors (Durkheim and Merton) and also research instruments: the anomie scales" (Besnard 1988: 94).

Besnard's analysis of the status and history of anomie sheds light on Merton's development of Simmel's *Übersehbar*. Like Durkheim's term, the notion *Übersehbar* in Simmel's work is largely undeveloped and unclear. Merton himself writes that Simmel "alludes" to the property of visibility, or that it was "obliquely and brilliantly introduced" (Merton 1957: 319). Part of the earlier identified conceptual confusion can be explained by this fact. Moreover, it appears that Simmel served an "emblematic function" in Merton's "Continuities" chapter, and especially in the development of his ideas on visibility. Merton's extension of Simmel's term served to symbolize and demonstrate the difference between those who stood on the shoulders of giants and those who merely, as Merton saw it, looked at them in awe (cf. Merton 1965).

There is evidence to suggest that, in Merton's view, the difference between these two attitudes toward the classics roughly paralleled the difference between functionalist empirical sociology and the Chicago School. On at least two separate occasions in *Social Theory and Social Structure* Merton reveals his attitude toward the Chicago sociologists.

In one of these instances, Merton contends "with only slight exaggeration," that the anticipations of reference group theory by William James, Charles H. Cooley, and George H. Mead, "remained almost wholly undeveloped for a generation or more" (Merton 1957: 278). This state of affairs was attributed to the uncritical acceptance of the words of these men as the "final words." Merton (1957: 278) explains:

> They were honored, not in the manner in which men of science do honor to their predecessors, by extending and elaborating their formulations on the basis of cumulatively developed problems and systematic researches bearing on these problems, but in the manner in which litterateurs honor their predecessors, by repeatedly quoting "definitive" passages from the masters' works.

While Merton does not say this, the sociological generation that followed the works of James, Cooley, and Mead was dominated by the Chicago School approach.

Our second example establishes a more explicit connection between differing attitudes toward the classics, on the one hand, and functionalism and the Chicago School, on the other. In an extensive footnote in the chapter of *Social Theory and Social Structure* titled "Patterns of Influence" (Merton 1957: 387–420), two approaches to the classics in general, and Simmel in particular, are noted. Once approach emphasizes the development of conceptions "in the course of emirical [sic] inquiry." By contrast, in the other approach, a thinker's observations and conceptions are merely reproduced. As an example of this second approach Merton mentions the Simmel translations by Albion Small published in the *American*

Journal of Sociology "during its early and impoverished years when American sociologists of intellectual taste were compelled to draw upon the intellectual capital of European sociologists" (Merton 1957: 404, note 13a).

As these two examples make clear, Merton's approach to the classics—represented by the saying attributed to Newton, "If I have seen farther, it is by standing on the shoulders of giants"—served to distinguish functionalist empirical sociology from the approach of the Chicago School. Merton's claim to have stood on Simmel's shoulders was a symbolic reminder of that difference.[6]

CONCLUSION

This chapter has examined Robert K. Merton's mid-1950s reexamination of Georg Simmel's writings. I argued that an understanding of this revisit must proceed on at least two planes of analysis. First, it is important to recognize that Merton's approach to Simmel was influenced by the perceived need to demarcate the boundaries between proper and improper uses of the classics. These approaches corresponded, respectively, with functionalist and Chicago School versions of sociology. Second, I showed how Merton's Simmel reception was influenced by a perceived need to resolve a social problem after World War II: the threats to democracy posed by the social structure of bureaucracy.

The "theory of organizations"—which occupied the attention of those in the two year-long seminars that served as the vehicle for Merton's Simmel revisit—was a code for those who were working on problems of society and democracy after World War II in America. Simmel's writings, then, were perceived to be relevant to the development of a theoretical perspective and a new, more democratic social order.

CHAPTER 6

THE HISTORICAL AND CONTEMPORARY IMPORTANCE OF COSER'S *FUNCTIONS*

INTRODUCTION

In a revealing interview, Lewis A. Coser commented that "the latent motives for doing much of my work are probably formed in the vicissitudes of my life and career" (Rosenberg 1984: 52). In addition, Coser has published several autobiographical writings (Coser 1988a: xi–xx; 1988b). Together, these publications can be taken as an invitation to pursue a contextualist interpretation of his sociological oeuvre. This chapter offers one modest contribution to such an undertaking: an examination of some neglected aspects of Coser's reception of Georg Simmel. Coser's dissertation-as-book, *The Functions of Social Conflict* (1956a), hereafter called *Functions*, will be the main focus of analysis.

It is the thesis of this chapter that Coser's reception of Simmel and his theory of conflict were a function of his reaction to the postwar loss of Marxist "revolutionary self-confidence and theoretical self-certainty"[1] and consequent search for new ideals and intellectual directions. It is basic to my argument that Coser's study on conflict was a deeply personal book and a historically situated statement. The following discussion will substantiate this biographical and historical argument and will draw implications for current sociological theory and research.

Lewis A. Coser was born in 1913, in Berlin, to Martin and Margarete (Fehlow) Cohn.[2] His father, a banker and stockbroker of German-Jewish heritage, did not himself attempt to assimilate, but changed the family name to Coser for the sake of his son. It is significant for his later intellectual career that Coser did not identify directly with his father's Jewish heritage or with the upper-middle-class background of his youth, but, rather with the cause of socialism and radical politics.

Still, Coser was to benefit from his father's economic situation and the educational opportunities it entailed. Following his father's wishes to gain international experience, he traveled to England in the early 1930s. He moved on to Paris rather than returning to Berlin in order to escape persecution by the virulent anticommunist campaigns of the ascendant Adolf Hitler. In Paris, Coser not only attended classes in sociology at the Sorbonne, taught by the aging Durkheimians Bouglé and Fauconnet, but also became intensely involved in radical political groups. One of these groups, a sect like Trotskyist organization, published a magazine called *Der Funke* ("The Spark"). About that group and its writings Coser remarked, "We were utterly convinced of the historical importance of our mimeographed papers" (Rosenberg 1984: 29).

The "revolutionary self-confidence and theoretical self-certainty" implied by that statement were not unique to Coser but were the privilege of an early generation of Marxists. Coser wrote as follows about this generation, and about himself, in the changed circumstances of the American mid-1950s:

> In the tradition in which men of my generation grew up, that is men who came to political maturity in the early thirties, radical thought was anchored in a view of history derived from, though not identical with, Marxist thought. *History moved, we felt, in some inevitable way* to a final eschaton in a classless society. Those who were committed to radicalism belong, they felt, to the vanguard of *the knowing servants of history . . .* their organizations . . . would help usher in the reign of freedom. (Coser 1956b: 157; emphases added)

Coser continued his discussion by characterizing the state of American radical political thought at that time. He expresses a palpable sense of loss of earlier confidence in the direction of history and in the certainty of theoretical vision:

> The situation in the fifties is profoundly different. Stalinism, Nazism, the decay of the labor movement in the West, have *shattered the certainties* of most of those who still claim allegiance to radical values. [According to] the rhetoric of the Marxism of the twenties and thirties . . . humanity marched forward and *we* knew its destination. But *most of us today have lost this faith in the possibility of knowing the inner logic of*

history . . . some of us have learned to discard the Hegelian hubris of "knowing" which sustained us for so long. (1956b: 157–58; first and last emphases added)

These comments are reproduced here not because they are thought to shed new light on the dissolution of Marxism from the 1930s to the 1950s (see Wald 1987). Rather they are included because they highlight so clearly Coser's *sense* of Marxism in decline; they provide evidence for his loss of "revolutionary self-confidence and theoretical self-certainty" at that time. This is not to imply, of course, that Coser was pessimistic about the future of radical thought. On the contrary, he was one of those intellectuals of the 1950s, too numerous to mention, who maintained their commitment to socialism and radical politics; who attempted to salvage the remnants of progressive thought; and who tried to foster the creative efflorescence of radicalism during that inhospitable decade. These commitments find an expression in *Functions*.

COSER AS CRITIC OF INDUSTRIAL RELATIONS

When selecting a dissertation topic, Coser did not set out to investigate a particular Simmelian text. His goal was more ambitious. He had initially proposed to write Simmel's intellectual biography, but was advised against the project by Robert Merton. Coser describes in this way the steps that followed the rejection of his initial topic:

I thought about the problem [of choosing a dissertation topic] and while reading Simmel's *Sociology*, which, of course, was not yet translated, I came upon the conflict chapter and got so excited that I said to myself, why not write a whole book on that? (Rosenberg 1984: 44)

Coser's selection of conflict as a topic signals his participation in a more general ground swell of postwar social thought and sentiment. Participants in this "movement" included: Daniel Bell (1947), Reinhard Bendix and Lloyd Fisher (1949), Herbert Blumer (1947), C. Wright Mills (1949), Harold Sheppard (1948; 1949), and Robert C. Sorensen (1951).[3] Despite the philosophical, theoretical, and political differences that may have existed among them, these thinkers all exhibited a number of commonalities. Four such points stand out: First, all of the thinkers listed above were reacting to what had come to be called "industrial sociology" or "human relations in industry." At the time, these phrases signified trends in thought and practice that were represented mainly, but not solely, by Elton Mayo and his school (e.g., Mayo 1933, 1946; Roethlisberger 1941; Roethlisberger and Dickson 1939; Whitehead 1938).

Second, the reaction of these individuals to the development of industrial sociology was overwhelmingly negative, although that negative judgment was often expressed in different ways depending on the thinker's perspective. On the one hand, Blumer's (1947: 272) main criticism seemed to be that the human relations in industry approach was largely irrelevant and unenlightening for an analysis of modern, dynamic industrial society. Mills (1949: 202), on the other hand, leveled his criticism against what he believed to be an ideological justification for corporate capitalism as expressed in the Mayo School studies. Blumer's liberalism and Mills's radicalism are evident in their differing, although not incompatible, concerns.

Third, all of these individuals were critical of what they believed was a largely anti-union bias on the part of Elton Mayo and the other representatives of "human relations in industry." Some of their own writings show evidence of a pro-union bias.

Finally, the reality of industrial strife was a concern of the members of this "movement." Most were critical of what they perceived to be a tendency on the part of Mayo and his fellow researchers to ignore conflict or, if conflict was acknowledged, to regard it overwhelmingly in negative terms. Bendix and Fisher (1949: 314) represent this outlook when they write, "It is difficult to understand Mayo's work unless one realizes how much he abhors conflict, competition, or disagreement."

All of these men recognized the reality of industrial conflict and some saw benefits flowing from the strife, but at least one contributor who wrote before Coser underscored the positive functions of conflict. Robert C. Sorensen ends his article, "The Concept of Conflict in Industrial Sociology" (1951), with an analysis of some of Simmel's ideas on conflict. He concludes with the following exhortation: "Ignoring the beneficial functions of conflict does a great injustice to any scheme of analysis industrial sociology may have to offer" (p. 267).

In sum, a number of individuals—to whom we shall refer as the "Industrial Sociology Critics," or Critics, for short—related by profession, by common interest, and sometimes by personal ties, created a collection of writings that was united in these three ways: (1) They were critical of Elton Mayo in particular, and his followers and others involved in industrial sociology in general; (2) They were pro-union; and (3) They were cognizant of and sometimes favorably oriented toward industrial strife.

Lewis Coser was a participant in this wave of intellect and sentiment. In view of the earlier discussion of his commitments, it is no surprise that he was inclined to add his voice to the chorus of criticism of industrial sociology. A self-professed opponent of social illusions,[4] he was certain to argue, along with Bendix and Fisher (1949: 318), that "the Goliath of industrial warfare cannot be slain by the David of human relations." Coser, a veteran of sect politics, was well equipped to reveal and assail the shibboleths (e.g., "spontaneous cooperation," "equilibrium") of the human relations experts. He was a radical committed to the ethical and political desirability of socialism; no doubt he could not countenance an approach to industrial relations that denigrated the worker and extolled the virtues of the manager.

Moreover, it is no surprise that Coser couched his criticisms in the language of sociological functionalism, in view of the sterility of the Durkheimian sociology that he encountered during his Sorbonne days, his insecure career in America as a political journalist, the defeat and enervation of the left movement in the immediate postwar decade, and the withering of his faith in Marxist theory and practice, discussed above. Coser believed that functionalism, especially the version of functionalism developed by Robert K. Merton, represented a new and revolutionary development of the field. Mertonian functional analysis offered Coser and many of his fellow students an intellectual spring during a political winter. "In those days at Columbia," he recalled, "it was a joy to be alive in a highly exciting intellectual atmosphere" (Coser 1988b: 68).

Functions as a Weapon in Social Conflict

Coser's dissertation, I believe, was the most systematic and farthest-reaching contribution to the literature of the industrial sociology critics. *The "theory of conflict" as developed by Coser can be considered, in one respect at least, as a dialectical alternative to the industrial sociology of the period.* If, according to the critics, industrial sociology provided a justification of the status quo, the theory of conflict highlighted the dangers of the times and underscored the importance of change. If, according to the critics, industrial sociology sided with or supported the perspective of management, the theory of conflict supported the unions. If the industrial sociologists emphasized the dysfunctions of conflict, Coser's theory of conflict highlighted the eufunctions of conflict—and so on.

It is my contention that Coser selected those parts of Simmel's text on conflict that he perceived as supporting the theory of conflict, so conceived. Selections from Simmel that supported those ends inadequately were extended by later theoretical and empirical developments. Occasionally he offered a creative misreading of Simmel—or misprision, in Harold Bloom's (1975) sense—in cases where Simmel's text was unsuited to what he perceived to be the needs of the historical moment. Coser read Simmel with strategic purposes in mind.[5] Among other purposes, he wanted to counter the conformist drift of industrial sociology. A functionalized Simmel then served as a weapon in the intellectual and political battleground of postwar America. I will substantiate these views with an analysis of the main arguments of chapter 3 of *Functions*, titled "Hostility and Tensions in Conflict Relationships" (Coser 1956a: 33–65). I selected this chapter because it introduces concepts central to Coser's arguments against conformist versions of industrial sociology.

In this chapter, Coser attempts to demonstrate theoretically the potential danger to individuals and social structures in a society intolerant of conflict. To this end, he presents two main conceptual developments: (1) the safety-valve theory of conflict, and (2) the distinction between "realistic" and "nonrealistic" conflict. In discussing both concepts he creatively misinterprets Simmel's ideas on conflict.

In the following passage cited by Coser, Simmel is said to offer a safety-valve theory of conflict:

> The opposition of a member to an associate is no purely negative social factor, if only because such opposition is often the only means for making life with actually unbearable people at least possible. If we did not even have the power and the right to rebel against tyranny, arbitrariness, moodiness, tactlessness, we could not bear to have any relation to people from whose characters we thus suffer. We would feel pushed to take desperate steps—and these, indeed, would end the relation but do not, perhaps, constitute "conflict." Not only because of the fact that . . . oppression usually increases if it is suffered calmly and without protest, but also because oppression gives us inner satisfaction, distraction, relief. . . . Our opposition makes us feel that we are not completely victims of the circumstances. (Coser 1956a: 39, citing Simmel 1955: 19)

According to this theory, Coser maintains, conflict "serves as an outlet for the release of hostilities which, were no outlet provided, would sunder the relation between antagonists" (Coser 1956a: 41). The hydraulic imagery Coser uses in this and other related passages—safety-valves, accumulation, blockage, release—is not only difficult to locate in the cited quotation from Simmel; it is also not consistent with Simmel's view of the origins of conflict. Simmel conceived the "hostility drive" as a priori: "It seems impossible to deny an a priori fighting instinct" (Simmel 1955: 29). According to Simmel, a priori drives are a part of human experiential equipment that shape experience (Weingartner 1962: 56–61; see also Oakes 1977: 23–24; 1980: 8–27). For example, the concept functions as an a priori in Simmel's sense when it serves "as a criterion by means of which certain contents are selected as belonging [to experience] and others are rejected as not belonging to it" (Weingartner 1962: 58). The "hostility drive" is such an operative principle for human emotional experience.

Simmel's language reflects this active, formative view rather than the hydraulic safety-valve theory of conflict set forth by Coser. According to Simmel, the hostility drive "seizes" upon those objects "which somehow appeal to it" (Simmel 1955: 33). Again, it might merely "add itself as a reinforcement (like the pedal on the piano, as it were)" to conflicts having more direct causes (pp. 33–34).

It appears that Coser presented a Freudian version of Simmel, at least in this chapter. Freud's concept of "id," however, is not consistent with Simmel's conception of the "hostility drive," as the foregoing discussion should make apparent. At the very least, no facile identification should be drawn between the two terms. Still, this creative misinterpretation served some useful purposes.

First, the safety-valve theory provided Coser with the means to identify and criticize those institutions that deflected radical potential away from "the struggle," the American workers' movement. In particular, he made reference to mass culture (boxing and wrestling matches on television, detective stories, daytime radio shows), which serves as "a general means of 'safe' release of aggressive drives which are tabooed in other social contexts" (Coser 1956a: 44).

Second, the safety-valve theory underscored the potential dysfunctions that await a society that relies on safety-valve institutions to dispose of accumulated aggressions and frustrations:

> Damming up of unrelieved or only partially relieved tensions, instead of permitting adjustment to changed conditions, leads to rigidity in the structure and creates potentialities for disruptive explosions. (Simmel 1956a: 47)

Third, the safety-valve theory provided the opportunity to introduce the distinction between realistic and nonrealistic conflict. The importance of this distinction is suggested by the substantial attention that the types of conflict have received (see Levine et al. 1976).

Coser is very clear in his justification for the creation of the new terms, realistic and nonrealistic conflict: the times demanded the distinction (Coser 1956a: 50–54). The terms were ammunition in the fight against the psychologization of "the struggle." According to Coser, workers fighting for higher wages through strike or union activity were being equated in the literature with frustrated individuals displacing onto their bosses their oedipal hatred toward their father. The distinction between types of conflict would help to avoid confusing these two dissimilar social types (p. 50). Furthermore, the distinction gave further occasion to contrast the theory of conflict with the perspectives of Elton Mayo and his followers and to criticize their failings. The following quotation is representative of this critique: "The studies in industrial sociology inspired by Elton Mayo . . . show a peculiar lack of sensitivity to struggles over power or pecuniary gains that arise in the factory" (p. 52).

CONCLUSION

Broadly stated, Coser's reception of Simmel, as represented in *The Functions of Social Conflict*, needs to be situated within the context of the dissolution of Marxism from the 1930s to the 1950s. More particularly, the book represents Coser's response to that disintegration and his attempt to identify new intellectual moorings for his critical impulses.

Examining Coser's book in this light reminds us that his theory of conflict was also a commentary on and weapon in the political and intellectual battlegrounds of postwar America. Coser was especially concerned with the implications of 1950s conformist styles of industrial sociology. In addition, the book reveals how creative and sometimes fertile misreadings of the sociological heritage become built into sociological theory; such errors are based not on faulty logic or evidence but on passion and concern for the future of democracy. Both Coser's famous safety-valve theory of conflict and his distinction between realistic and nonrealistic conflict were formulated strategically to correspond to the political needs of the time.

Of what particular importance for present theorizing are these observations? In the present context, some suggestive leads must suffice.

In *Theories of Civil Violence* (1988), James B. Rule charts the shifts in theoretical attention that sociologists have given to collective violence. These shifts are explained more accurately by the changing estimations of a theory's political worth, he argues, than by estimations of a theory's scientific worth. The dustbin of conflict theory past contains an array of potentially useful concepts, perspectives, and propositions. From Rule's point of view, scientific merit should matter more in contemporary theoretical work than it did in the past.

If Rule is right in believing that the great challenge facing conflict theory in particular and social theory in general is the taming of political and other passions by science, a revisit of *Functions* has contemporary relevance. Coser's attempt to balance a "double career" (Coser 1988b) as social critic and scholar, however successful or unsuccessful, provides a salutary lesson for those sociologists whose calling is similarly troubled.

PART THREE

Simmel as Modernist and Postmodernist

INTRODUCTION

Between the years 1890 and 1920, three men—Max Weber, Emile Durkheim, and Georg Simmel—made significant and lasting contributions to sociological theory. These three scholars devoted their intellectual lives to explaining the troubled changes in economy, society, polity, and psyche that accompanied the emergence of modern, industrial societies. Simmel's contribution to the study of modernity was early and decisive, earning him the title, in David Frisby's words, of "first sociologist of modernity." His later writings reveal sufficient parallels to the work of contemporary postmodernists that he has also been called "the first sociologist of postmodernity."

Part Three includes two essays that chart the varied reception of Simmel's work along the themes of modernity and postmodernity. The first essay by Albert Salomon, a student of Simmel and Weber, acknowledges but criticizes Simmel's modernity. Quoting the words of Goethe's Faust, Salomon refers to Simmel's work as "bad and modern." Salomon admired Simmel's sociological analysis of the Jews, but criticized his "soft" reasoning and psychologism. In contrast, the work of Weinstein and Weinstein, discussed in the final chapter, embraces Simmel's modern and postmodern qualities. Two worlds and two worldviews divide the convictions of these authors. Salomon was an émigré from Germany who narrowly escaped the Nazi death camps, who embraced the belief that reason was the best weapon against tyranny, and who suffered the insults of modern society, including the low estimation of intellectual labor. The contemporary postmodernists, in contrast, distrust the tyranny of reason and rationality. Fueled by a sort of cultural radicalism, they reject the straitjacket of cultural rationality and embrace cultural fragmentation, iconoclasm, and subjectivism as liberating. In Simmel they believe they have found an ally.

While they disagree over the value of the modern-postmodern impulse in Simmel's work, the authors share a common admiration for Simmel's support for human liberation. Indeed, it is probably this shared conviction that unites all of the authors examined in this book. Simmel's writings have provided inspiration and guidance to generations of men and women who are supporting progressive causes, fighting tyranny in all its forms, and advancing the frontiers of sociological thought. It is likely that Simmel's work will continue to provide such support in the future.

CHAPTER 7

GEORG SIMMEL RECONSIDERED, BY ALBERT SALOMON[1]

Edited, with an Introduction and Notes by Gary D. Jaworski

In the limited collective memory of sociology, Albert Salomon (1891–1966) is remembered primarily as a Weber scholar. It is true that he was a part of the Weber circle at Heidelberg, where he received his Ph.D. in 1921. It was this affiliation, as well as his friendship with Karl Mannheim and progressive political views, that formed the basis for Alvin Johnson's invitation to Salomon to join the faculty of the University in Exile, later to become the Graduate Faculty of Political and Social Sciences of the New School for Social Research. In addition, Salomon's essays on Weber in the first volumes of *Social Research*, the New School's house journal, helped not only to introduce generations of students to the themes and methodology of Weber's sociology; they helped to solidify Salomon's reputation as a Weberian. But as even a cursory review of Salomon's publications would show—especially of his books *The Tyranny of Progress* and *In Praise of Enlightenment*—he was a scholar with a wide range of interests and competence. His deep engagement with French social and philosophical thought, not only with Durkheim and the Durkheimians but with Montaigne, Montesquieu, and Malebranche as well, reveals another dimension of Salomon's thinking. His legendary courses on Balzac and on the sociology of the emotions reveal another.

It should come as no surprise, then, that Salomon would give his attention to the writings of Georg Simmel. If one casts a wide net, one is likely to catch some big fish. But Salomon's interest in Simmel was not just a consequence of the catholicity of his intellectual tastes; he was once Simmel's student. Like many others from his native Berlin and from around the world, Salomon sat in one of the big lecture halls where Simmel lectured and witnessed the master at work. The encounter was not an altogether positive experience, however. He was both attracted to and repelled by Simmel: attracted to the questions he asked and the manner of engaging those questions; repelled not only by Simmel's appearance (he found Simmel to be physically unattractive) but by his modernity. Salomon's rationalism, his faith that through reason one can grasp the whole truth, clashed with Simmel's psychologism, intuitionism, and other concessions to the modern revolt against reason.

Salomon brought his knowledge and conflicted appreciation of Simmel's writings to his New School courses, where Simmel was featured not only in history of sociology review courses, but in regularly offered seminars on Simmel, from the 1940s through 1966, the year of his death, as well as in a unique course comparing the writings of Simmel and Alfred Schutz. Besides the lecture notes and syllabi to those courses, there are few written records of Salomon's engagement with Simmel's work: a brief entry on Simmel in *The Universal Jewish Encyclopedia* (Vol. 9, 1943) and a few pages of his chapter on "German Sociology" in Gurvitch and Moore's *Twentieth Century Sociology* (New York, 1945). What follows is an essay that presents Salomon's most developed and detailed reading of Simmel.

"Georg Simmel Reconsidered" was presented January 9, 1963, to a small but erudite audience at the Leo Baeck Institute in New York City. Siegfried Kracauer, himself a student of Simmel's, was in the audience and participated in the ensuing discussion (see the brief description of the event in the *LBI [Leo Baeck Institute] News*, Spring 1963, p. 1). While one can only guess at the issues that were debated then, the paper is notable now in a number of respects. Along with establishing that Salomon was Simmel's student and confirming earlier reports about Simmel's teaching style, the essay convincingly defends Simmel against his anti-Semitic detractors. More important, Salomon uses these attacks as an opportunity to advance a powerful sociological analysis of national patterns of anti-Semitism and the role of the Jew as Other, to employ contemporary language. But there is more. He undertakes a critique of Simmel's essay on the stranger, a critique that anticipates later analyses and advances original arguments of its own. The analysis of *une maladie eternelle*, a version of "the return of the repressed" derived not from Freud but from Montesquieu, is as valid today as it was when it was first formulated. In sum, there is much to be gained by reading this essay today: as historical document, culture critique, and sociological analysis.

—Gary D. Jaworski

In 1910, I attended for the first time classes at the University of Berlin. I remember vividly the lecture course Simmel gave. In the widest classroom, which stretched from the Southside of the university with a view to Unter den Linden to the Northside looking over the old chestnut trees to Dorotheenstreet, he lectured at the godless time from 2 to 3 P.M. in order to deter the hundreds of people who crowded his classes. He was disgusted with the fact that he was fashionable; but even at such an hour, there were hundreds of listeners in the largest classroom of Berlin University. Unforgettable was the impression of his personality. He was physically unattractive. When he began to speak, he was fascinating and repellent alike, as if surrounded by a halo of solitude and disgust. He really did not address the audience in the reciprocal give and take of a good teacher; he was talking in a monologue. His words came from somewhere, from an opaque experience like lightning, shocking and fascinating alike. He seemed to be a stranger, an adventurer in ideas and an actor whose gestures, of his hands in particular, feigned the spontaneity of his thinking in class, while he probably performed the same gestures every time he gave the course. Throughout my reading of Simmel's works and later in my teaching Simmel, I never got rid of the ambivalent reaction of fascination and repulsion.[2]

Georg Simmel was born in Berlin in 1858 at the corner of Friedrichstrasse and Leipzigerstrasse. His parents belonged to the higher ranks of the middle classes; they were already converted and Georg was baptized into the Christian community. The topographical remark is a symbol of Simmel's mentality. He was and remained the product of a metropolitan civilization, overwhelming through a variety of sensual, intellectual, technological, poetical, and artistic impressions that had their impact on the future author of the "Sociology of the Senses" and of the analysis of the metropolitan structure and intellectual life. He lived under the horizon of subjective and objective culture implying a sentimental attitude toward nature.

Yet Berlin was a spot that had all the conditions for inspiring a potential sociologist. Individuality had a rare chance to articulate itself in the merry-go-round of societal contacts and relationships and in the meetings of diverse social worlds: Christian, Jewish, academic, artistic, literary, journalistic. It was a place to encounter many different perspectives and structures. People could be social and alone, unfolding their selves in inner independence at the expense of social conformism. This topographical condition of his growth and life was one of the sources of his future sociological studies, which were never separated from his philosophical concerns. He became a philosopher sociologist, one and indivisible. But the climate of this spatial frame of reference had no impact on Simmel. He did not have the slightest spark of Berliner humor. The inner independence and trust in some good ending that gave Berliners the sovereignty of being relaxed even in defeat and the belief that *uns kann keener*[3] was completely absent from Simmel. He could be ironical, witty, and cynical, but he completely lacked the serenity and freedom that are conspicuous in humor. His was an unshakable seriousness in spite of the possibilities of great tenderness in human and aesthetic responses. In an autobiographical remark, he stated that he felt fortunate that he grew up in a historical situation of radical transformations in which Nietzsche and Marx, Naturalism and *l'art pour l'art* shook all dogmatic positions in philosophy, social sciences, and aesthetics.[4] He felt an affinity to the new antimechanistic biology and vitalistic philosophy and psychology of Bergson. It is surprising that he did not mention Schopenhauer in this context. As a matter of fact, he stated in his book *Schopenhauer and Nietzsche* that Schopenhauer's philosophy of will was a greater stride forward in philosophy than Nietzsche's conception of life.[5] Simmel's own conception of life is a strange merger of Schopenhauer and Nietzsche in his formula that life is more life and more than life: more life as growth and evolution, and more than life as the transcendence of life in the act of free and creative reflection on the life process itself and on the human personality beyond the pale of social roles.

Simmel studied at Berlin and finished his Ph.D. in 1881; he became a *privatdozent* at the same university under Dilthey in 1885. In the second edition of the *Einleitung in die Geisteswissenschaften*, Dilthey admitted Simmel's conception of sociology as a genuine contribution to philosophy and social sciences, referring to his own historical-sociological categories in the book mentioned.[6] Though Dilthey was an implacable anti-Semite, he sponsored Simmel's habilitation. Simmel remained in this position until 1901 when he was nominated *ausserordentlicher professor*, a title which did not make him a member of the faculty.

A call to Heidelberg was prevented by a report of Windelband to the minister of education in Karlsruhe in which the term "destructive" as describing Simmel's thinking played a basic role. How far Windelband's own anti-Jewish feeling was involved, is unclear. I am definitely prejudiced against Windelband because he was responsible for the death of Emil Lask, the only potentially great and original philosopher in the philosophy department of Heidelberg. He was killed in action as a soldier in World War I because Windelband refused to request his return to Heidelberg as indispensable to philosophy. Emil Lask was a Jew.[7]

In his note to Windelband, the minister probably referred to a rather emotional and excited letter he had received from Dietrich Schaefer, a medievalist at the university of Berlin. His letter was an outcry against a scholar of whose descent and origins he pretended to be ignorant.[8] His emotional outburst sounded the alarm for the intellectual health of the German students who, he believed, were being exposed to debunking, analytical, and empty methodological thinking, a process of thinking that moved in the vicious circle of reflecting on its own reflection without solid and final results. Simmel finally received a full professorship at the University of Strassburg in 1914. He died in 1918 after having finished what was probably his one surviving book written under the shadow of death: *Lebensanschauung*. This book will remain when all the others are forgotten.

EVALUATING SIMMEL'S ANTI-SEMITIC DETRACTORS

In our context the relevant problem is a sociological one: the positive and negative reciprocity of so-called Jews to native populations. Simmel was legally not a Jew. When he was of age, he left the Protestant church to which he belonged and remained outside all ecclesiastical institutions. He never called himself a Jew, nor did he ever identify himself with this minority. The violent anti-Jewish revolt against Simmel's way of thinking, therefore, claims an examination. First, is this presentation true, is the entire mode of Simmel's philosophizing destructive, or is it misrepresented? Second, is there anything like Jewish ways of thinking in philosophy and in the sciences?

Regarding the first question, I wish to state that the scope of Simmel's reflection goes beyond the "destructive" trend of thinking that he shared with Marx, Nietzsche, and Schopenhauer. Simmel added to his historical relativism and sociological perspectivism a positive attitude toward art, a position completely in the traditions of Schopenhauer. According to Simmel, men can reach the absolute and divine in the production and reception of art. Art is the true redemption from life, the genuine synthesis that closes the dualism of scientific and philosophical reasoning. Rodin's work in sculpture was to Simmel a manifestation of the divine in artistic perfection. It is difficult to call a philosopher destructive who continues traditions of aesthetic philosophies.

Nor was his discovery of the domain of the social a negative conception. On the contrary, to articulate the specificity of societal relationships, as distinguished from individual psychology and moral philosophy, was of greatest relevance for the study of the depth layers of human nature. Simmel conceived of the new discipline as dealing with reciprocal human interdependence—as social roles in social structures; he pointed out the dynamic perspectivism that recreated continuously the dynamism of social structures. He analyzed in his sociological essays the merry-go-round of the social stage on which the typical patterns of social roles were mixed up with the contingencies of the commedia dell'arte and possible adventures of life. There is nothing destructive in the analysis of the conditions under which people attempt to realize specific goods or are prevented from achieving them. On the contrary, sociological thinking is an indispensable aid to practical behavior in the concrete situation. It can teach us to weigh the relationships between means and ends in the context of a social structure and to consider the expectations of our fellow human beings. In the establishment of the new field of sociology, Simmel followed Dilthey's suggestions to study human beings as the juncture of the totality of historical conditions. Simmel continued the idea by constituting humans as the sum total of social roles and a unique personality beyond the pale of social roles.

These observations stress the error of the academic attack on Simmel on the grounds that it is anti-Semitic. Schaefer and Windelband conceived of Simmel's qualifications according to the image of a Jew that they took for granted. This is a genuinely sociological problem. It belongs to the intellectual and emotional economy of societies to divide the worlds in which they live according to the images they form or have inherited from their ancestors. Men and women construct their worlds as they build up a game of chess—as a universe of friendly and hostile alignments. Such imagery depicts the division of society into friendly and hostile, positive and negative relationships, and into fields of neutrality that might be friendly today and inimical tomorrow. Human beings, according to their *Weltanschauungen*, might have a positive or negative evaluation of the military or of the business, an optimistic conception or a pessimistic appreciation of bureaucracies or civil service.

Furthermore, we live by images or counterimages of, for example, the Russian and the English, the Egyptian and the Algerian, the Chinese and the Purme. We learn and are indoctrinated with such images since our youth and throughout the stages of our education in schools, in the army, and in our profession. For most people, the normative pictures of our social roles are taken for granted. Among such pictures is the image or counterimage of the Jew. While the value moment of the ideal images changes with changing social structures, the image of the Jew remains identical as that of the stranger. The Jew is a stranger, the counterimage to the native community; the Jew is the image of Judas to the Christian; or the mysterious merchant, the usurer, the cheater to the hard working farmer, worker, bureaucrat. The Jew was to the relaxed leisure class a tool for satisfying their uncommon requests for precious goods and financial help.

The merger of these images continued through the Western world with some variation, though, in general, immutable. The German academics inherited such images in the traditions of their class and society, of their political and ecclesiastic affiliations. It might have been merged with the care of their vested interests. When they encountered Jews in the flesh, they often found that they did not correspond to the images. The professors declared that these Jews were exceptions or they had the phrase, "You like to make fun of me," when a candidate introduced himself as a Jew.

The Prussian Junkers met with Jews as businesspeople, indispensable as cattle and corn dealers. Such relationships in which nothing human or personal came to the fore influenced their conception of the Jew as a grim Shylock; they absolutized such generalizations and were quite embarrassed when meeting with cultured Jews. The military carried an ineradicable image of the Jew as physically and mentally not good material for the army, regardless of concrete cases to the opposite. Stereotypes of the Jew as escaping the front-line service for office work in the hinterland or for government work at home belonged to World War I anti-Jewish propaganda, a pillar of Hitler's success. The petit bourgeois, including the social-democratic masses, shared in the national prejudices against the Jews. The most dangerous anti-Semitism was the brooding hatred of the lower-middle classes conceiving of Jews as unscrupulous, voluptuous, cowardly, and shrewd. In particular, the white-collar workers, declining middle classes, were the most favorite classes for Hitler's propaganda (Kracauer!).[9] Hitler was from Braunau in the German Sudetenland, but he received his anti-Semitic training in Vienna, where the Lueger type of radical anti-Semitism was the violent response of frustrated classes against successful Jewish advance on the social ladder.[10]

Though Simmel was not a Socrates, the accusations against him are the typical reproaches of all traditionalists and reactionaries against innovators: to corrupt the youth. That the Jews should be singled out as such corrupters of the youth belonged to the academic pattern of anti-Semitism in Germany. I might remark that the case of Simmel has its parallel in France. The same radical anti-Judaism ruled the French academic and conservative groups at the same time. The rise of sociology and moral science in the works of Durkheim and Lévy-Bruhl was received by the ecclesiastical and reactionary elements in the Third Republic exactly like Simmel's work in Germany—as destructive, radical, and threatening to the academic standards of moral and religious philosophy. In England the problems were different. The most independent social classes, such as the highest ranks of nobility, could be relatively free from traditional social pressures. Erwin Panofsky often quoted one of his intimate friends, a man of old feudal descent, as saying: "We can only have friends among our peers and cultured Jews, we do not have friends among the bourgeoisie." Such casuistry was, of course, unusual. In general, Christian and social prejudices were taken for granted.

While Simmel's writings do not exhibit the destructive tendencies claimed by his anti-Semitic detractors, they do reveal genuine limitations. Simmel's shortcomings are, first of all, in the philosophy of history and the related writings. He believed that he could construct its methodology with the device of psychology without regarding the historical existence of man as a basic element of historical knowledge. It was the tragedy of Simmel that he never stuck to his philosophical intentions but always escaped into psychology. All his books dealing with philosophy of history are frustrated because he conceives of the discipline in terms of psychology. Heidegger, though fascinated by Simmel's last book as making a genuine contribution to a philosophy of human existence, regretted that Simmel remained in the ontic-psychological area and never succeeded in arriving at the ontological concepts which he had in mind.

But the main weakness of Simmel's thinking appears in the lack of radical reason, in his desire to enjoy variability and the infinite potentialities of human self-realization in their existence here and now. Simmel's deficiencies lie in his modernity. His work deserves the Faustian reproach, "Bad and Modern, Sardanapal."[11] This is Simmel: craving for an escape from scientific reasoning, logic, and social causality into the fields of sentimentalities, intuitionism, and psychological ambiguities that carry no coercion. Simmel had forgotten that the great ages of rationality produced thinkers, theologians, and philosophers—Christian, agnostic and skeptics—who, because they were rationalists, were able to penetrate and illuminate the total human situation in its opaqueness through the swinging arch of constructive consciousness. Montaigne victoriously transcended the decay of his physical living toward death with the *quand même* of reason and a challenging love of life in spite of all.[12] These deficiencies are just Simmel's property and are not shared by all of the thinkers with whom he shared relativism and the anarchy of values.

The second question that requires an answer is the following: Is there a mode of Jewish thinking beyond the specific dialectical thinking that results from the study of Talmud and Midrashim? Is there anything Jewish in the thinking of Marx or Friedrich Julius Stahl in spite of their Jewish self-hatred. Is there a specifically Jewish trait in Simmel's microscopic sharpness, concentration, and in the abstractness of his analytical or synthetic essays? Though I am deeply convinced that a comprehensive interpretation of a philosophical text should begin with a consideration of the linguistic and literary structure, I do not find any sparks of such a Jewish style. What seems to many readers a stylistic Jewish device in Marx, the changes of subject into predicate and vice versa, is a literary tool frequently applied by Jean Paul. Authors are primarily conditioned by their teachers, they gain their literary style in the revolt against old masters and in the experience of new perspectives and new moods.

Simmel's style of thinking and writing is more influenced by Schopenhauer than by Nietzsche; in his methodological writings the influence of Rickert is evident; in his intellectual biographies, such as on Goethe, Rembrandt, and Kant, he is influenced by the prose of these authors transformed by the intensity of his mind, which penetrated the totality of their thinking. Ortega y Gasset called him a philosophical squirrel apropos the book on Goethe.[13] All these conditions merged in a stream of soft and sharp phrasing that expressed his process of thinking, a process that was rarely logically tight, but often followed casual associations through metaphors and imagery. The style of Simmel's thinking and writing was that of a *precieux triste, jamais ridicule.*[14]

SIMMEL'S ANALYSIS OF THE JEWS

Simmel treated the problem of the Jew in the Western world three times as a historical and sociological concern. The philosopher of individuality, to whom the meaningful uniqueness of the personality was the highest value, faced a situation in which certain individuals were not recognized as individuals, were refused to be admitted as equal fellowmen, but were just tolerated as patterns of strangeness, strangers, outsiders—exoteric phenomena excluded from the communion of belonging.

In the *Philosophy of Money*, Simmel referred to the pariah situation of the Jew during the Middle Ages as imposed on them by the Christian princes.[15] They equipped the Jews with a monopoly on money lending, a practice that was incompatible with the moral teaching of the Church for Christians. This was a pragmatic device to exploit the international family relationships of the Jews for financial arrangements in a still agricultural and market-town economy, an economy that needed such merchant relationships for more refined goods and the anonymous, impersonal money power. A part of the persecution of the wealthy Jews was a matter of expropriating their financial goods; the other type of persecution was directed against the poor Jews because they did not live up to Christian expectations. The first crusade was nothing but a pogrom in Southern Germany and along the Danube (Simmel does not say anything about that). The Jew became a part of society, a stranger in a homogeneous group. Montesquieu saw the general problem of politically negative privileged minorities almost in Simmel's perspective. The Armenians in Turkey overcompensated their status as second-class citizens by accumulating economic wealth by trade and commerce, which made them indispensable to the Turkish Sultan. Montesquieu implied the same pattern for Jewish minorities and their value for the monarchs, many of whom had their own Jewish bankers (as did the great houses of the Polish nobility).

This passage in the *Philosophy of Money* historically anticipates the sociological treatment of the Jew in the chapter on the self-preservation of the group in *Soziologie*.[16] Simmel dealt here first with stable and fixed social establishments, like armies and police forces of a body politic. But he suggests that stability of social organization is not a good by itself. The value of social institutions is relative to the function they fulfill in the totality of the social field. Even the state requires dynamic and flexible forces in the secret police fighting spies and criminals.

There are always conditions for certain groups that require flexibility, elasticity, and the readiness for dynamic action on a moment's notice. Such are criminal gangs, revolutionary conspiracies, and gypsies. From the gypsies his associations carry him to the Jews, whose precarious existence forced their alertness from day to night and night to day. He admired the stubborn identity of their collective self-shining through the coercive migrations, sudden departures, and involuntary adventures. He quoted what people said about the Jews—it is remarkable that he is always able to discover the most anti-Jewish sources for his demonstrations (the author might be Konstantin Frantz): "The strength of the social cohesion of the Jews, the feeling of deep solidarity, the special though vanishing exclusiveness toward all non-Jews—all their social bonds of close interdependence, it is said, may have lost their religious coloring since the emancipation, but gained instead the capitalistic chain. For this reason, it is said, 'the organization of the Jews is invincible; for, as soon as the hatred against the Jews would deprive them of their power over newspapers and capital, even abolish their status as citizens, the association of Jews would only lose its social and political organization; it would be reborn in its original religious institutions. Such a social-political game has occurred here and there locally; it might be repeated at large.'"[17]

Simmel uses the description of such a collective pattern in order to explain the unbelievable flexibility of the Jew in accommodating to all changes in his life conditions. Simmel thinks that the variability and versatility of the single Jew in adjusting to all changing conditions (and the dynamic ability to grasp the most diverse assignments) are the result of the structure and horizon of his traditional life among strangers, as a stranger himself. In this sociological context, Simmel dares to make correlations between such life situations of Jews and their lack of creative genius in poetry and the arts, on the one hand, and their preeminence in the performance of great works in the theater or on the concert stage, on the other. It seems to me that such a sociological correlation is unwarranted. The creative role of Jews as philosophers, mathematicians, and scientists demonstrates simply that in the historical traditions of the Jews the arts simply did not play the role that intellectual discipline and rigid reflections exerted on the continuity of strict mental work.

Finally, Simmel made a sociological analysis of the stranger in the context of the chapter on space and its relevance for societal relationships.[18] Space is meant as a fixed condition of living and as a symbol of social structure. The opposite pole is the wanderer, aspiring for freedom from all fixed points in space. Simmel distinguishes two types of strangers. First is the wanderer who comes today and leaves tomorrow. These are the nomads and tribes departing from old homesteads and migrating for a long time before finding a new settlement. All inter- and supernational civilization during the Middle Ages and in the Jet Age belongs to this type. During the Middle Ages, clerks and knights, professors and students, poets and monks were at home in Sicily and England, in Paris and Bologna, in Bagdad and Cairo, in Venice and London. In antiquity, the sophists and orators were wandering strangers earning their living by moving from place to place and teaching the future politicians the arts of statecraft. In the honeymoon days of capitalism Gaudissart, though at home in Paris, is the first traveling salesman: the embodiment of the myth of optimistic capitalism.[19] Among sociologists, many of the researchers are certainly contemporary sophists and are wanderers when invited or required. There are many economic nomads in the age of technological unemployment.

But Simmel is not interested in the patterns of nomadic existence. His problem is the stranger who comes today and remains tomorrow. We call such a man in plain sociological terminology an immigrant. Simmel would have had a tremendous material for studying the phenomenon. Thousands of Russian Jews emigrated with the Hamburg-America line year by year to escape the pogroms organized by the Russian police. For them immigration to the United States was heaven indeed. Regardless of voluntary or coercive emigration, the immigrant is a stranger to the native populations, who speak another language, live by habits, mores, and social conventions that they take for granted in the routine of everyday life, and have their own codes of behavior, from manners—what to do with the napkin after a meal—to their system of relevances—priority of economic success over political or intellectual prestige.

My late distinguished friend Alfred Schutz wrote a moving essay on "The Stranger," based on the personal experience of being a stranger as immigrant to the United States.[20] It was a sociological analysis of the time process required to adjust the immigrant to the prevailing behavior patterns and to make him a conformist, the process of turning the stranger into a native. It remains, however, a question whether the transitional immigrant should be termed "stranger."

Simmel defines the stranger as the person who comes today and remains tomorrow. In contrast to the optimistic description of the immigrant stranger by Schutz, Simmel interprets such life situation as a social fixation with the potential departure for another home. In other words, the stranger resolves to settle at a specific place with the reservation of moving again. In the posthumously published *Fragmente und Aufsätze*, edited by G. Kantorowicz, I found the following reflections: "The deepest desires of our life: to depart from home, to embark upon traveling and to arrive at a (new) home, being and becoming."[21] This remark indicates the deep affinity of the stranger to the adventurer, both referring to Simmel's philosophical pattern. Simmel himself took it for granted that as a stranger he was an adventurer of the mind, departing from home and its shelter on open roads or the wide sea of the spirit in order to arrive at a new home, the result of his own decision. But the potential of new experience and ventures remained: the philosopher's privilege to reconsider his ideas and to reexamine them in the light of new situations of his life.

CRITICAL COMMENTARY ON SIMMEL'S STRANGER

The stranger who decides to settle in a social context experiences the grim fact of not belonging to these people, not sharing their traditions and recollections, their intentions, and the horizon of meaning they take for granted. The stranger carries qualities, experiences, and ideas that derive from a former life situation as nomad, migrant, or traveling salesman. Simmel maintained that the reciprocity of closeness and distance that is contained in any situation appears here in the following constellation: distance in the role of the stranger means that closeness is strange, while strangeness means that the strange is near. It is Simmel's contention that the role of the stranger is a special case of reciprocity. Simmel repeatedly insists that the stranger is an element of the organic group, though an inorganic appendix. The paradox of the Simmelian stranger is the dynamic unity of inside-outside, of esoteric-exoteric. He calls the situation of the stranger a positive reciprocity. On the contrary, it is my considered opinion that the situation of the stranger is hell! Shakespeare, who knew everything, was better informed than Simmel.[22]

Furthermore, I disagree with Simmel when he suggests that the stranger has the same position in the context of society as do the poor and the radical. The poor and the radical do not feel the distance to the group that the stranger logically and necessarily has, nor does the group respond to them as they do to the stranger. Charity belongs to the system of social obligations, the poor is part of the whole. The political radical, though critical toward the social status quo, acts for the sake of complete identification with the truth of social order.

Simmel takes his historical casuistry from the preindustrial world in which the peddler-merchant fulfills the function of conveying precious goods, jewels, silk, and spices to agricultural and market civilizations. The people know that the strangers will come sometime during the year. They will be familiar and strange, liked and disliked, loved and suspected. When such wandering businesspeople decide to settle, they are going to function as traders, financiers, bankers. Simmel in his metaphorical language calls such figures supernumeraries, a term that leads him to refer to the history of the European Jews as classical example of the stranger. Jews remain the strangers whatever they might have done to the people of their establishments. They are by race, by religion, by occupation, by law a people who are different from the natives. They might love the social context in which they settled—the language, poetry, music, and art—but their own contributions will be reproductive rather than productive. Simmel correlates this phenomenon to the formal-technological thinking as required by their specific business as financiers or bankers.

It has been stated quite frequently that the essay on the stranger is an autobiographical statement of the precarious situation of the Jew in the Western world. The historical casuistry taken from a premodern model does not make this thesis convincing. Simmel knows that other foreigners and strangers were the founders of international banking. Lombars and Florentines, the rich in Antwerp, Huguenots in exile, Quakers and Pietists—all were businesspeople and sometimes through their economic wealth great political powers. Simmel knows all the historical cases; unfortunately, he refers in *The Philosophy of Money* to the formal concept of *money*, while he intends to speak of capitalism, banking, and financial, not industrial, capitalism. In comparing the premodern to the modern economic world, he states the exceptional place of the Jewish moneylender and merchant in the premodern society, while they are the common phenomenon in the modern financial and capitalistic worlds. There is a passage in *The Philosophy of Money* that recalls a statement by Marx in *"Zur Judenfrage"* ("On the Jewish Question")—that the emancipation of the Jews means that all men have become Jews under and through the modern economic system. Simmel, of course, simply stated that the unique position of the Jews as financial businesspeople in the Middle Ages had vanished with the rise of capitalism and a class of bankers, national and international. In spite of such internationalization of the big financial enterprises and the social intercourse of Jewish and Christian bankers at the top of the social ladder, the Jew remained a stranger and outsider on all social levels, as mentioned before.

Simmel mentions as a positive contribution of the stranger his objectivity, a result of his distance and affection alike. It goes without saying that this kind of criticism from the outside is never appreciated by any group. The members of the traditional group reject the idea that such well-meant suggestions will meet the true requirements of their historical group. Simmel is wrong to call objectivity the quality on behalf of which judges from other places were called on by the republics of the Renaissance in Italy. They were invited because of their reputation of fairness and equity, not because they were uninvolved in the partisan prejudices of local politics.

Furthermore, Simmel identifies a phenomenon with the stranger that is actually the role of the anonymous. But there is a fundamental difference. We might confide to a taxi driver or to a fellow traveler on a long trip personal experiences, joys, and worries because they are nobodies; we would not talk like that to a stranger. There is still another societal relationship wrongly inserted in the essay: alienation of lovers is not strangeness nor does it turn them into strangers. Such confusion belongs to the sloppiness of Simmel's process of thinking.

Simmel's definition of the stranger is unsatisfactory, sociologically and ontologically. The stranger is a person who lives in the world as if not really living in it. The world of everyday life, the social world, is as strange to the stranger as it is to the people who live by their social roles for the fulfillment of social goals. The reciprocity of strangeness derives from the fact that the stranger is either from the outside a foreigner or from the inside a philosopher, that strange creature who lives by the intention that philosophy *necesse est, vivere non*.[23] The philosopher and scientist are indeed the true strangers in the social world in which human beings and institutions are directed toward securing present and future pragmatically for themselves and for their offspring. The philosopher and the scientist have selected the contemplative life, dedicated to the truth about the whole. For this reason the common people always made and will continue making fun of the philosopher. The Greeks pictured Thales the stargazer as a fool who exposed himself to ridicule when falling into puddles.

Montesquieu observed that common people are always suspicious of philosophers, mathematicians, and scientists as potential heretics, magicians, and sorcerers. Montesquieu intimated that the true stranger is the philosopher who lives in critical distance to his society. Such behavior enables the stranger to penetrate and illuminate the total behavior of human beings—their follies and ambitions, their vanities and superstitions, their virtues and vices. The stranger is qua philosopher the most lucid sociologist. Such interdependence of sociology and philosophy has been considered indispensable by Merleau-Ponty. The philosopher is the called-for guide for foreign strangers who wish to understand a civilization unknown to them. The philosopher is the very thinker who reflects on the social roles of Persians and Jews, questioning the finality of such conceptualization. The philosopher's thinking is directed toward the problem of whether there is a humane self, a *humanitas*, beyond the pale of

Christian or Jewish institutions, beyond *nationalitas*, beyond *religiositas*. Simmel's mode of thinking moves between George Herbert Mead and some problems of a philosophy of existence.

Simmel and Montesquieu, both, know the inner affinity of the stranger and the adventurer who disrupts the routine of everyday life, who leaps into the experience of something beyond the stereotypes of life before returning and bowing under the yoke of daily obligations. Both philosophers shared in specific life experiences. Simmel never stated in his writings his attitude toward the humiliation and offenses to which he was subject. *Totum se dedit*: to his work and to its maturing.[24] Like Simmel, Montesquieu passed through frustrations and disappointments in social life, in his marriage, in the hopes for a diplomatic career. He retreated to his mansion and found comfort and strength in his philosophical work. He continued the tradition of Montaigne in the concern with the total human situation and he elaborated on its historical variation.

Montesquieu was the only post-Christian thinker who had some grim sympathy with the Jews. Grim was his affection because he was radically anti-Christian, a new Stoic philosopher. For this reason he could not forget that the Jews had inaugurated Christian religion. He once scribbled in his notebook that the Jews could relax, for they would no longer be persecuted for their religion's sake. He left it open what other motives would be invented. In *The Spirit of the Laws*, Montesquieu invented the letter of a converted Jew to the Spanish and Portuguese Inquisition.[25] This letter is a flaming and indignant outcry against the persecution of the Jews and the *autos-da-fé* of extermination. The Christians themselves degrade and corrupt their religion by such procedures, they expose it to the reproach of hypocrisy and fiction.

Montesquieu knew too well from his study of man in history that all over the world there exists *une maladie eternelle*. This sickness consists in the recurrent social law that majorities and minorities, suppressed and humiliated for centuries, will once emancipated render their accumulated resentments with interests, in order to overcompensate the wounds of their suffering. Montesquieu formulated the law apropos the destruction of the Roman Republic by the emancipated masses of the people, who succeeded through their tribune of the people in establishing the military dictatorship that ended in the institution of the Principate by Augustus. This resulted in a new tyranny supported by the wealthy bourgeoisie and the decay of the traditional Roman political aristocracy of the nobility of office.

This rule is valid for majorities and minorities alike. It is valid for the behavior of the German Jews after their emancipation.

Though limited in the careers open to them, they displayed skills, efforts, and talent to rise and be superior to the traditional classes in the economic and cultural fields. Such Jewish advance took place against all odds of stubborn resistance and silent sabotage. For this reason, the Jews had to muster their highest accomplishments in order to be admitted, for instance, to the academic world, which normally would have been quite satisfied with the mediocrities of inbred academic families.

The German anti-Semites took it for granted that Jewish intellectuals were active in liberal and socialist politics and journalism; they forgot however, that Friedrich Julius Stahl, the intellectual who wrote the Tivoli Program for the Prussian Conservative Party, was a converted Jew like the radical Karl Marx. It is a symbol of the scope of Jewish thinking that the conservative and radical ideologies should have been phrased by men whose descent was Jewish. Stubbornness in remaining true to the authority of traditions and to the traditions of authority belongs to fundamental Jewish attitudes as much as the radicalism that derives from absolute criteria for moral and social conduct.

It goes without saying that the remarkable achievements of the emancipated Jews increased the anti-Semitism in connection with social and political constellations. In January 1918, I attended a party, where only Jews were present: religious, zionist, agnostic, atheistic, and pragmatic Jews. There was one topic of conversation: how to get into the political or administration offices of the Federal or Prussian governments after the breakdown of the imperial regime at a time when anti-Semitism was rampant. I felt disgusted and remember to have said: "It might be good for the articulation of the Jewish character and for the strength of Jewish dignity when we would be back in the Ghetto." The Eternal Malady moved in the vicious circle of pressure, overcompensation, and increased pressure toward the catastrophe of 1933.

For Simmel, whose philosophy is centered around the value of individuality as meaningful personality, the phenomenon of the stranger remains and perseveres in the generality of an image or counterimage respectively. For this reason, Simmel's conception of the combination of nearness and distance in the social context reveals his secret idea. The strangers who settled in a land that is not their own might be able to love such elements in the social and cultural structure that articulate their individuality, that make them grow and mature in their very personalities. Such personal accomplishments confront the unceasing distance of stereotyped images or counterimages of the native societies. Simmel advanced the thesis that strangers might be tied to others (only to lose their individuality) in occupational, professional, and political groupings. This is nightmarish to Simmel. In addition, he is alarmed by images of the stranger as the villain who destroys the affectionate bonds uniting ruler and ruled. In the perspective of the kings and subjects, the reciprocal patriarchal affections of father and children can only disintegrate through courtiers and ministers who, as strangers to the affectionate communion of king and people, ill advise the good king for their own selfish interests. Likewise, the ruler can imagine revolt and revolution only by the villainy of foreigners and strangers, who seduce the loyal subjects in the interest of their own self-aggrandizement.

The best case for the ambivalence and ambiguity of the concept of the stranger as a sociological category is the Latin notion *hostis*, that is, the political military adversary and at the same time the guest looking for shelter in the face of death. We all live in the communion of suffering; we all have and are limits in the finiteness and transcendence of the human situation. . . .[26]

CHAPTER 8

SIMMEL AND THE
AMERICAN POSTMODERNISTS

IS SIMMEL A POSTMODERN THINKER?

As the foregoing chapters show, each generation of American sociologists appropriates some aspect of Georg Simmel's writings for its own needs. In the 1930s Simmel's writings on formal sociology helped Talcott Parsons forge a definition of sociology with theoretical and practical consequences. By advancing the frontiers of action theory, sociologists could at the same time help mend the growing rift between the spiritual and economic orders. By midcentury, Lewis A. Coser was fashioning Simmel into a functionalist in an effort to add a lively and critical balance to an increasingly conformist polity and profession. Later, in the sixties when the United States was anything but balanced, the sociologists of everyday life found in Simmel's *lebensphilosophie* and microsociological talents the intellectual grounds for social and sociological insurgence.

The current Simmel revival eschews these earlier interpretations of Simmel and his work. The definitions of Simmel as a formal sociologist, as a functionalist, and as a microsociologist are deemed unenlightened and unenlightening. Moving beyond these views, many contemporary sociologists view Simmel more broadly as the first sociologist of modernity (Frisby 1985), and more recently as the first sociologist of postmodernity (Stauth and Turner 1988: 16). These new definitions are based on the mutual need for a founder's myth on the part of those social theorists who are seeking to rebuild a new social order (modernity) and those who are seeking to continue breaking down the old social order (postmodernity).

This chapter examines efforts to appropriate Simmel for postmodern social theory. It explores the warrants and the problems of identifying Simmel as a postmodernist; and it proposes a resolution of some of these problems.

By what justification can Simmel be called a postmodernist? Four preliminary answers can be discerned: the contextualist, the perennialist, the divinationist, and the contemporanist gambits.

In the contextualist approach, there is no justification for identifying Simmel as a postmodernist. There is an irremediable gap between the past and the present, between modernity and postmodernity. Simmel wrote at a time that is not ours, engaged in disputes that have long been abandoned, and confronted issues that no longer exist using intellectual conventions that have changed. Consequently, an interpretation of Simmel's works is possible only by situating the texts in his historical context and understanding them in terms of his problems not ours. To interpret Simmel's writings in terms of our postmodern concerns would be to commit the error of presentism, reading the past through the lens of the present.

The perennialist gambit offers an answer that is, in one sense at least, opposite to the one provided by the contextualist. If the contextualist contends that Simmel's relevance is ephemeral, the perennialist maintains it is abiding. Like other great thinkers, from Plato and St. Augustine to Marx and Heidegger, Simmel addresses eternal questions in the universal language of reason. He can shed light on our postmodern problems because they are not unique to us, but are contemporary manifestations of the eternal problems of humankind. For example, Simmel directed his brilliant mind to the dilemmas of freedom and individuality, problems that help to constitute the human predicament (Levine 1971). It is this quality in Simmel's writings that entitles him to be considered a classical sociologist and his writings to be included in the classical canon; and it is this quality that permits us to identify Simmel's thought as relevant to postmodernity.

Neither of these answers can be acceptable to postmodern interpreters of Simmel. The first, contextualist approach is reductionist and renders impossible efforts to interpret Simmel as a postmodernist. If there exists an irremediable gap between past and present, and if we exist on the far side of that gap, then Simmel cannot speak to our concerns. The second, perennialist approach is objectionable to current philosophical and moral predispositions, such as to the postmodern embrace of relativism and diversity and the corresponding rejection of the rationalist pretensions to universalism. Given the eschewal of these alternative responses by contemporary analysts, the two remaining answers are relied upon to justify Simmel's putative postmodernity.

The divinationist view holds that, because of his unusual brilliance and great sensitivity to vital cultural currents, Simmel was able to anticipate our postmodern problems and perspectives. This answer concedes to contextualism the point that Simmel's time is not our time; but it counters with the argument that thinkers can transcend their time and advance ideas congruent with some other historical era. Simmel was such a thinker. The other answer rejects the contextualist view that Simmel's time is over by offering a contemporanist answer to the question. Simmel is our contemporary and is addressing in his work, or some portion of it, the same problems we now face. By resolving the hermeneutic problem of temporal distance, these two positions grant epistemological warrants to efforts of interpreting Simmel as a postmodernist. The divinationist holds that a thinker's special abilities of foresight mediate the temporal distance between the past and present. The contemporanist, by contrast, offers no such mediation since it denies the existence of temporal distance.

Weinstein and Weinstein (1989; 1990a; 1990b; 1991; 1993) have presented the most sustained, if unsystematic, attempt to date to appropriate Simmel for postmodernism. Using at times the divinationist gambit and at others the contemporanist gambit, they attempt to establish the grounds for their views, efforts that are courageous yet shifting and indeterminate, like the postmodern world they purport to analyze.[1]

FLÂNEUR OR BRICOLEUR: CONTRASTING IMAGES OF SIMMEL

Weinstein and Weinstein (W & W) are perceptive advocates of the relevance of Simmel's social thought to postmodernism. In the essay, "Simmel and the Theory of Postmodern Society," W & W (1990b) criticize the contextualist challenge to Simmel's postmodern appropriation and offer in its place a divinationist approach. Contextualism, they argue, "performs the salutary function of preventing misplaced abstractions, but it often fails to grasp the significance of a thinker for future generations" (W & W 1990b: 75). Because contextualism emphasizes the embeddedness of thinkers in their historical context as well as the uniqueness of historically specific discursive formations, it "tends to neglect fruitful anticipations" (W & W 1990b: 75). Such anticipations come about when thinkers "push beyond the confines of their era" and foresee "the problems which will preoccupy future reflection" (W & W 1990b: 75). Granting Simmel's contribution to the discourse of modernity, W & W nevertheless insist that he is also and more importantly "a pathfinder beyond it" and is "struggling painfully beyond it" (W & W 1990b: 76, 77).

Not all of Simmel's writings anticipate postmodernist discourse. According to W & W, the breakthrough to postmodernity can be found in Simmel's late works on culture, especially in "The Crisis of Culture" (Simmel 1976b [1917]) and "The Conflict of Modern Culture" (Simmel 1976a [1918]), the "Conflict" essay being one of Simmel's last statements on his times.

In "The Crisis of Culture," Simmel analyzes the predicament of his age within the framework of his problematic of the tragedy of culture. In this problematic, which recurs through many of his essays on culture, from *The Philosophy of Money* (1900) to "The Crisis"(1917), the advancement of objective culture exceeds the ability of individuals to appreciate and internalize those cultural objects for their own subjective benefit. As objective culture advances, perfecting its forms at the expense of personal accessibility, subjective culture declines for want of continuing sustenance from fresh and accessible cultural forms. This situation results in a crisis in which individuals and groups attempt to dispense with form altogether through rampant subjectivism, empty activism, and ultimately nihilism.

According to W & W, while Simmel is painfully aware in this essay of the agony, fragmentation, and paradox of "modern/postmodern society" (W & W 1991: 169), an awareness that qualifies as an anticipation of postmodern discourse, he has not fully broken through the confines of his times or modernist theoretical problematics. One reason is that the essay exhibits the nostalgia and cultural pessimism of his generation, especially when Simmel grants the possibility of retrieving elements of a lost cultural unity, as when he writes of efforts to "salvage the values of the former life from the collapse of their forms and carry them over into the new life" (Simmel 1976b [1917]: 260). Another reason is that the essay provides a modernist escape clause in the concept of life. To quote W & W (1990b: 81):

> In "The Crisis" life and form are held in tension with each other in a "process of interaction"—they are not antithetical forces but are defined reciprocally in terms of the polarity flux and fixed, each one a necessary moment in the totality of the life process . . . Life itself, as form-giving activity, is not problematized and, thus, can be dogmatized, can remain a repository of hope for spontaneous renewal.

In "The Conflict of Modern Culture," however, Simmel transcends both the nostalgic impulse of his time and the metaphysical optimism of his earlier philosophy of life. It is in this text that he abandons the problematic of the tragedy of culture and presents a new problematic of cultural deconstruction. Simmel presents cultural history as "the story of the replacement of one central idea by another over time, but it has no unifying central idea of its own" (W & W 1990a: 351). Simmel's identification of a "never-ending change in the content of culture" (Simmel 1976a [1918]: 224) extends to the realm of culture Marx's insight into the succession of economic forms. But for Simmel there is no final eschaton to which history is heading. Rather, it "moves between the poles of death and rebirth, rebirth and death" (Simmel 1976a: 224). This absence of a historical metanarrative renders Simmel's thought "far more in tune with current postmodern thinking" (W & W 1990a: 351–52), with its "incredulity to metanarratives" (Lyotard 1984: xxiv), than with the thought of his own time, with its nostalgic search for a lost unity. Moreover, at the end of "The Conflict" Simmel negates any possibility of salvation from the conflict in modern culture; life is now engaged in a radically negative project—to deconstruct itself. To quote Simmel (Simmel 1976a [1918]: 225):

> We are at present experiencing a new phase of the age-old struggle, which is no longer the struggle of a new life-imbued form against an old, lifeless one, but the struggle against form itself, against the very principle of form.

These features of Simmel's discourse—its reading of cultural history as deconstruction, its rejection of metanarrative, its abandonment of metaphysical optimism—all render Simmel's discourse "contemporaneous with our own cultural situation, which gives us the privilege of understanding him more fully than the previous generations have been able to do" (W & W 1990b: 77).

W & W supplement these efforts to appropriate Simmel for postmodernism with efforts in revisionist image-making. They substitute for Frisby's (1981) modernist image of Simmel as a *flâneur* for the intelligentsia the postmodernist image of Simmel as a *bricoleur*. This effort is only the latest in a line of iconographic construction of "Simmels," a series of images in which are charted the hopes and fears of three generations of sociological critics.

In the sixties, Lewis A. Coser (1965) fashioned an image of Simmel as a "stranger in the academy," a view that accorded well with the sentiments of academic Marxists prior to the radicalization of the university later in that decade. According to this view, Simmel's scholarly nonconformity, theoretical disorderliness, and intellectual originality can be accounted for, in part, by his marginal position in the German university system. Simmel was in but not of the academy; his prolonged status as a *privatdozent*, fifteen years as an unpaid lecturer dependent on student fees, drove him to look beyond the academy for support and encouragement. Simmel found compensatory rewards in the applause of his nonacademic audience, a form of encouragement that fostered both his own intellectual innovation and alienation from his academic peers. This image of Simmel as a "stranger in the academy" manifested not only Coser's own conflicted position as social critic and scholar (Coser 1988b; Jaworski 1991); it also expressed the fear and the consolation of academic radicals before the events of 1968: the fear of career failure and the consolation of intellectual profundity.

By the early eighties these radicals had become assimilated into an academy that was characterized by declining enrollments and conservative retrenchment. A new image of Simmel was created to accord with this troubling reality—Simmel as *flâneur*. Following Baudelaire (1964) and Benjamin (1973), Frisby (1981) characterized the *flâneur* as a detached observer of modern urban life who wanders through the world at a distance recording observations in the form of pleasing but harmless portraits of the social scene. Simmel's propensity for the essay form, his penchant for ambiguity and paradox, his interest in the fleeting and fragmented aspects of city life, all accord with the character of the *flâneur*. These traits in Simmel's writings, argues Frisby, derive from Simmel's position as a member of the powerless educated bourgeoisie in Wilhelmine Germany. Lacking confidence in their abilities to shape that society, these intellectuals, and Simmel in particular, retreated to the interior of their salons and psyches and offered pleasing but harmless and convictionless portraits of modern life (Frisby 1981: 83).

In this image of Simmel the domesticated radicals of the 1980s would have not only a new way of thinking about Simmel; they would have a mirror of themselves as well. Frisby (1981: 166) drew the connection between Simmel's time and his own when he writes in the final paragraph of his book:

> The critical interpretation of Simmel's social theory [offered in this book] should not lead one to conclude that his is the only theory that is permeated by the weakness of an aestheticisation of reality. The reader might also recognise whole traditions of sociology that have and do share this apparent

detachment and aesthetic perspective, particularly those that are preoccupied with constructing sociology as a self-enclosed perspective.

While Coser alerted the radical community to the consequences of academic marginality, Frisby warned of the consequences of academic success. With marginality came intellectual originality; with success, the academicization of Marxism, came intellectual and political sterility (cf. Attewell 1984; Jacoby 1989).

Recently, W & W (1991) have rejected this characterization of Simmel as a *flâneur* and substituted a new image of him as a sociological *bricoleur*, an image for the postmodern nineties. Frisby's earlier characterization is charged with being ad hominem, since the word *flâneur* is pejorative; inappropriate, since Simmel did not use the word to describe himself; ungrounded, since the basis for the image, say W & W, is not Simmel's work but commentary on that work by Simmel's contemporaries; and inaccurate, since it is inconsistent with what Simmel actually wrote (W & W 1991: 151–60).

This critical analysis is offered as persuasive grounds for rejecting the view of Simmel as *flâneur* and substituting an alternative image of him as an intellectual *bricoleur*, or a thinker who combines existing materials in new ways to complete the task at hand. The word *bricoleur* derives from the social thought of Lévi-Strauss (1966), who drew an analogy between the practical *bricoleur*, a handyman or jack-of-all-trades, "someone who works with his hands and uses devious means compared to those of a craftsman" (Lévi-Strauss 1966: 16–17), and mythical thought, "a kind of intellectual *bricolage.*" Like the practical *bricoleur*, who uses available objects to complete his task, the constructor of myth takes from the treasury of finite and heterogenous ideas the units from which new mythical structures are ordered and then reordered. Following this line of analysis, W & W characterize Simmel's essays as all so much bricolage, creative combinations of "the stock of culture that is given to him in his social environment, and the psychological and existential responses that are generally made to it" (W & W 1991: 162). Moreover, each essay constitutes an "aspectival totalization" (W & W 1991: 162), that is, it illuminates an aspect of the totality, not the totality itself, which, given the built-in incoherence to postmodern life, cannot be rendered. Like mythical thought, which lacks a final, all-encompassing super-myth, so Simmel's thought includes "no totalization of totalizations . . . no meta-narrative, and no deep structures" (W & W 1991: 161).

In this revisionist iconography of "Simmel" are revealed the sensibilities of the contemporary postmodern critics. Expressing neither the confident opposition of the "stranger in the academy" image, nor the distress of the retreatist and convictionless *flâneur*, the image of Simmel as *bricoleur* expresses the happy complacency of those who have come to believe that "vital solipsism" (W & W 1990a: 354) and lack of convictions are entirely appropriate responses to the postmodern condition. W & W (1991: 167) make this point stating:

> It is doubtless that the modern self is afraid of the gratuity of any commitment with reference to its historical meaning, that is, of not knowing which side will win or even if the struggle has yet to be decided. But historical gratuity is the grace of the postmodern condition, the opportunity to be a *bricoleur*, to construct a self and strategy of living from the shards of objective culture.

W & W question whether the convictions that Simmel is alleged to have evaded are even possible in a postmodern world (W & W 1991: 159). Rather than being a political retreatist and neurasthenic *flâneur*, as Frisby (1981: 80) maintains, Simmel may have been "simply sane and lucid" (W & W 1991: 161).

A CRITIQUE OF POSTMODERN(IZED) SIMMEL

Despite the care with which these views have been argued, they do not hold up under close scrutiny. Problems can be found not only with the specific warrants for claiming Simmel for postmodernism, but also with the more general theoretical views within which those claims are made.

W & W consistently argue that Simmel anticipated current postmodern theory. This divinationist gambit, as I have called it, is a riposte to the contextualists' claim that Simmel's time is not our time and that he should be understood within the context of his own culture, audience, and theoretical problematics rather than in the context of ours. In contrast to this point of view, W & W maintain that Simmel escaped from his time by anticipating the problems that now preoccupy us. Since these problems we now face are postmodern, Simmel's writings are relevant to current postmodern concerns. This argument has serious flaws that should produce grave doubts about its plausibility.

W & W do not explain in any satisfactory way how it is that Simmel was able to perform this intellectual feat. That is, how could

Simmel, writing in the years before his death in 1918, anticipate not only our current culture wars but also the intellectual perspectives by which we make sense of these battles? Was Simmel projecting into the future the problems he then faced; was he positing a future in the form of a hypothesis or was he prophesying the future through special gifts of divination (cf. Bell and Olick 1989)? While W & W never clearly specify which, if any, of these processes are at work, they come closer to the latter approach when they refer to Simmel's "great sensitivity," his "brilliant intellect," and his efforts of "struggling painfully" beyond his time (W & W 1990b). While this interpretation may be appropriate to the task of iconography, portraying a man with superhuman powers and extraordinary courage, it is hardly appropriate to the task of scholarly analysis. Instead of answering the problem of the basis for Simmel's anticipatory gifts, this answer merely relocates the problem to the murky realm of the psychology of genius, a secularized version of divine inspiration.

The rationalist use of the word "anticipation" does not result in the problems associated with divinationism. This is because rationalism does not interpret anticipation as a mental property of a thinker, but as an intellectual property of a concept. Anticipation refers to a degree of resemblance between a prior concept and a later concept. As articulated by Merton (1967), *rediscovery* refers to later discoveries that are substantially similar to earlier ones, *anticipation* applies to earlier concepts that overlap somewhat with later ones, and *adumbration* refers to even smaller resemblances between earlier and later formulations. These distinctions are developed within an image of science modeled on the natural sciences. Such a view maintains that there exists an objective world "out there" to be discovered, and that scientific knowledge is the incremental and progressive approximation of concept to that world. It is well known that postmodernism does not share these assumptions. It may be submitted that W & W sought to distance their argument from this rationalist framework by redefining anticipation psychologically. However, this divinationist gambit leads to the difficulties discussed above, problems that the rationalist model, which has its own difficulties, does not share.

Another problem with their argument is its general lack of internal consistency. W & W jointly maintain two contradictory premises. The first is that "there is no essential Simmel, only different Simmels read through the various positions in contemporary discourse formations" (W & W 1991: 153). This premise entails the conclusion that there can be no privileged interpretations of Simmel, for there are no discourse-independent facts that might adjudicate among differing interpretations. The second premise is that because many contemporary analysts now live Simmel's problematic, they have "the privilege of understanding him more fully than previous generations have been able to do" (W & W, 1990b: 77). But this second premise contradicts the first one by turning the present standpoint into a privileged point of access to Simmel's work. As a result of these inconsistencies, their interpretation collapses.

Other problems can be found with their use of the contemporanist gambit, the argument that Simmel is relevant to current postmodern concerns because he is our contemporary. W & W conflate two different forms of contemporaneity. The first, existential contemporaneity, denotes the sharing of similar life space. As Schutz wrote, "The social world of contemporaries (*soziale Mitwelt*) coexists with me and is simultaneous with my duration" (Schutz 1967: 142). The second, conceptual contemporaneity, refers to the sharing of similar theoretical assumptions and tools. Obviously, these two forms of contemporaneity do not imply one another. Existential contemporaries may adhere to differing conceptual systems, and conceptual contemporaries may live in different historical eras. One need not be an existential contemporary of Plato's to be a Platonist. W & W have not separated out these two forms of contemporaneity to the detriment of their analysis. This difficulty comes out most clearly in the following quotation:

> "*The Conflict*," which is the most unique and original work in Simmel's canon, *pushes beyond the parameters of his other writings*, leaving off from the past and breaking entirely new ground in its profound acknowledgement of the positivity of modernism and of its essential failure: in this text the postmodernist discourse erupts. *In "The crisis" Simmel is still a representative,* though certainly not a typical one, of his generation, though he is struggling painfully beyond it. *In "The conflict" he is contemporaneous with our own cultural situation,* which gives us the privilege of understanding him more fully than previous generations have been able to do. (W & W 1990b: 81)

In the italicized sections of this passage, Simmel the man, his discourse, and sociocultural reality dissolve into one another. While this may be sloppy writing, I believe it expresses a more fundamental error, that of conflating existential and conceptual contemporaneity, a confusion that renders their contemporanist argument vague and indeterminate.

This conceptual muddle results from a more general failure in much of postmodern social theory—the reduction of economic, political, and social issues to questions of cultural dynamics. When reality is assumed to be constituted by signs and discursive formations, the necessity for careful conceptual discrimination between concept and existence is lost. As Vidich (1991: 138) has observed about Baudrillard's *America*:

> Having as his aim an attempt to capture the spirit of America as revealed in its simulacra preordains his story to be one that ignores fine distinctions or discriminations. Baudrillard fails to attend to the social heterogeneity of a complex country, one whose society is made up of a vast aggregate of multi-ethnic, religious, racial, class and status groups.

W & W manifest this same failure in their essay discussed above, "Simmel and the Theory of Postmodern Society" (W & W 1990b). Not only do the authors neglect to present a theory, in any acceptable sense of the term, of postmodern society; they fail to either define or discuss the dimensions of such a society. Elsewhere, W & W conceive of society as "a tangle of tightly and loosely coupled syntagmatic chains" (W & W 1991: 160), that is, as series of signs signifying one another apart from their external referent. With such a conception of society, W & W are liberated from the burden of fine conceptual discrimination between words and referents.

Indeed, the entire project of demonstrating, through both the divinationist and contemporanist gambits, that Simmel is relevant to current postmodern theory is misguided and unnecessary. It is misguided because it remains entangled in the "metaphysics of presence" (Derrida 1974), the search for foundations, from which W & W seek to escape (W & W 1990b: 85). Their project is based on two questionable assumptions deriving from such a metaphysics. The first is that postmodernism is a temporal term, referring to a specific historical period after that of modernism. The second is that Simmel must *be* in our time, whether through intellectual foresight or temporal coevalness, in order for his thought to have relevance. Together, these assumptions attempt to provide a point of privileged access to Simmel's thought, a view that was shown above to be inconsistent with their postmodern relativism. Their project is unnecessary because when both of these assumptions are discarded, an argument for Simmel's postmodernism can be made that is free from the problems with their analysis.

AN ALTERNATIVE VIEW OF SIMMEL'S POSTMODERNISM

Rather than conceiving of the postmodern as a specific historical period, it can be considered a philosophical mode. This shift of
definition lies behind the recent efforts of Koelb (1990) and his colleagues to evaluate the grounds for Nietzsche's postmodernism.
Koelb observes that Lyotard did not define postmodernity historically but philosophically, as "incredulity toward metanarratives"
(Lyotard 1984: xxiv). These views are unmistakably recorded in
Lyotard's (1991: 34) recent work as well, such as where he writes:

> Postmodernity is not a new age, but the rewriting of some of
> the features claimed by modernity, and first of all modernity's
> claim to ground its legitimacy on the project of liberating
> humanity as a whole through science and technology.

On the one hand, does a thinker offer a metanarrative, an integrating
story such as the story of human liberation mentioned by Lyotard? If
so, such a thinker is characteristically modernist. On the other hand,
if a thinker offers no master story, and if his or her work subverts the
possibility of such a story, then the thinker can legitimately be called
a postmodern thinker.

Koelb (1990: 4–5) suggests that Nietzsche may be considered
postmodern in this philosophical sense. His deconstruction of the
self-legitimating rhetorics of science and philosophy; his
"incredulity" toward the liberating benefits of historiography; and
his recognition, through an appreciation of Greek philosophy, of the
profundity of the superficial—all qualify Nietzsche as a postmodernist. Such an argument is made not by claiming for Nietzsche
contemporary status or special powers of foresight, but by demonstrating that Nietzsche's thought radically undermines the possibility of metanarrative. While W & W have rightly identified the
absence of metanarrative in Simmel's cultural theory (W & W 1991:
161), they do so within an indeterminate and inconsistent framework. By abandoning the historical and adopting the above philosophical definition of postmodernity, more defensible grounds for
their claim of Simmel's postmodernity can be established.

Oakes's (1977; 1980) writings on Simmel's theory of form
clearly establish Simmel's postmodernism in this philosophical
sense. While he does not use the term postmodern, Oakes nevertheless reveals that the premises guiding Simmel's theory of forms
radically undermine totality, closure, unity, and privileged stand-
points. As summarized by Oakes (1980: 26–27), Simmel's forms may

be represented as distinct but impermanent and incomplete lan-
guages, deriving from life, which function as conditions for the possibility of representing the world. The universe exhibits a plurality of
such forms, such as the *Weltformen* or universal forms—science,
religion, art, philosophy—each one of which providing a legitimate
and incommensurable "take" on reality.

In this view, science cannot claim status as a privileged language. While Heidegger's *Geworfenheit*, or "thrownness," for example, may not be true in any scientific sense, this condition does not
result in the term's inadequacy as a philosophical expression. The
reason is that the criteria of truth and falsity that legitimately apply
within the realm of science may not be the criteria appropriate to
evaluating a philosophy. Each form has its own characteristic language, its own internal standards of evaluation. It follows that good
science, good art, and good religion will offer different but equally
legitimate modes of experiencing and conceptualizing the world. In
an analysis of Simmel's form, Oakes (1980: 86) concluded:

> Simmel's theory of forms entails that any given conceptual
> scheme can only have an incomplete, fragmentary, and transi-
> tional status. It follows that these properties must also be
> ascribed to Simmel's own conceptual apparatus. Under these
> conditions, it is not surprising that Simmel was sometimes
> inclined to describe his enterprise in language which suggests a
> journey that has no end.

Oakes's analysis of Simmel's theory of form is consistent with
W & W's analysis of Simmel's cultural theory. Both recognize the
partial and incomplete or fragmentary nature of those forms. But in
one important respect, at least, their analyses differ. W & W, on the
one hand, contend that Simmel's breakthrough to the postmodern
occurred in his late writings on culture. Oakes (1977; 1980), on the
other hand, has demonstrated Simmel's incredulity to totalizing
metanarratives through analysis of two of Simmel's earlier texts,
"On the History of Philosophy" (1904) and *The Problems of the Philosophy of History* (2nd ed., 1905), and of his later philosophical
essays, "The Problem of Historical Time" (1916), "The Constitu-
tive Concepts of History" (1917–1918), and "On the Nature of Historical Understanding" (1918).

Whether Simmel's turn to postmodernism in the philosophical
sense can be identified in his earlier philosophical writings, as
Oakes's work suggests, or in his later writings on cultural theory, as
W & W maintain, is a question that can be decided by others. What

is certain is that Simmel's philosophy was an expression of his life and times, a mode of being shared by his predecessor Nietzsche, and perhaps by his successors, the contemporary postmodernists.

This redefinition of postmodernism has the merits of fostering a fidelity to postmodern premises and promoting a broader consensus on Simmel's postmodernism. Its fidelity to postmodern premises is gained by abandoning the substantive and temporal understanding of the term. As Lyotard (1991: 25) has observed, "Historical periodization belongs to an obsession that is characteristic of modernity," with its promise of liberation through overcoming, renewing, or fulfilling the past. As such, the temporal definition of postmodernity is tied to the very grand narrative schemes which the philosophical definition holds suspect. Moreover, and again following Lyotard, the periodization of cultural history into pre- and post- "leaves unquestioned the position of the 'now,' of the present from which one is supposed to be able to achieve a legitimate perspective on a chronological succession" (Lyotard 1991: 24). But such a now is "impossible to grasp," since it "never stops fading away" in the flow of consciousness and the course of life (Lyotard 1991: 24). By detemporalizing postmodernism, the philosophical definition avoids both of these difficulties.

In addition, this redefinition can promote a broader consensus on the issue of Simmel's postmodernism. It has already been established that Oakes's explication of Simmel's theory of form supports Simmel's postmodernism in the philosophical sense. The opportunity exists to expand this support. The redefinition may ease Frisby's reluctance to grant Simmel's postmodernism, an unwillingness that already shows signs of waning. Frisby (1991b: 90) once was disinclined to admit Simmel's postmodernism, assigning him at most to the "prehistory" of postmodernity. He has more recently shown a willingness to accept the notion that Simmel's work anticipates, in the rationalist sense, postmodern theory, although he gives no support to the contention that Simmel is a postmodern theorist (Frisby 1992: 169).

This latter position is based on two premises. Frisby relies on a contextualist argument of intention: "Neither Simmel nor, for that matter, Nietzsche or Benjamin set out to develop a theory of postmodernity" (Frisby 1992: 168). In other words, since Simmel did not intend to commit a postmodern social theory, he cannot legitimately be identified as such. Those scholars who seek to claim that Simmel is a postmodern theorist are repeating the error of presentism; their claims "must be recognised as the activity only of contemporary commentators" (Frisby 1992: 168). But this argument cannot be sustained. It fails to recognize the legitimate argument, forcefully advanced by Simmel himself, that an account of a theory can never be exhausted by an account of a theorist's intentions. As Simmel (1980: 114) precisely stated the case:

> The relationship between the creator and his work invariably betrays this rather curious property. The autonomous artifact contains elements that cannot be explained by reference to the intentions of the artisan: additions, deletions, something of greater value, something of more modest value.

Frisby also relies on a substantive and temporal understanding of postmodernism, as "an extension or accentuation of tendencies already present in . . . modernity itself," or as "a new face of modernity" (Frisby 1992: 169). This view moves close to the claim that Simmel anticipated postmodern concerns, while at the same time lending no support to the claim that Simmel *is* a postmodern theorist. But if we detemporalize postmodernism, Frisby's reluctance thaws. For he accepts Simmel's postmodernism in the philosophical sense when he identifies neo-Kantian philosophy generally, and Simmel's work particularly, as precursors to Lyotard's definition of the postmodern condition as the abandonment of grand narratives (Frisby 1992: 169).

By further developing a consensus on Simmel's postmodernism, we can avoid unnecessary internecine battles over questions of Simmel's image and identity, and focus our efforts on the mutual exploration of Simmel's contribution to understanding modernity, postmodernity, and beyond.

NOTES

CHAPTER 1

1. Consider, by way of contrast, the important study, "Simmel's Influence on American Sociology" (Levine, Carter, and Gorman 1976). For over two decades now, this key reference has provided the best portrait of Simmel in America. And yet, if the details of that study have held up to closer scrutiny (e.g., Jaworski 1991), the limitations of its approach, noted by Wolff (1977: 226), still stand: "The person or human being who was interested in [Simmel's writings] unfortunately and characteristically remains unexamined; products are treated as if they were of interest only detached from the producer."

2. Lindsay studied in Berlin in the spring of 1892, mainly with Wagner, and in the same year took his Ph.D. at Halle. Thilly studied philosophy and psychology in 1887–1889 at Berlin and then for two years at Heidelberg, where he took his Ph.D. in 1891. Walter Goodnow Everett, a Brown Ph.D., studied at the Universities of Berlin and Strassburg in 1895–1996. Charles Montague Bakewell, a Harvard man who spent most of his academic career at Yale, studied at the Universities of Berlin, Strassburg, and Paris in 1894–1896. Information from various editions of *Who Was Who in America*.

3. For a useful review of Simmel's works in translation, see Frisby (1991a). Most of the *AJS* translations were by Albion Small, with the exception of "The Sociology of Religion." Charles A. Ellwood obtained Simmel's permission to translate and publish the piece (Ellwood to Small, 20 August 1904, Albion W. Small Papers, Box 1, University of Chicago). He gave the job to William W. Elwang, a minister and student of his who, with Frank Thilly, the Cornell philosopher and reviewer of Simmel for *The Philosophical Review*, would subsequently translate Friedrich Paulsen's *German Universities and University Study* (Paulsen 1906).

4. I would like to thank a reviewer for pointing out that Simmel himself did not share Small's insistence on "correct beginnings" or secure foun-

dations before embarking on scientific work. "Simmel argued to the contrary," the reviewer writes, "that scientific work on general questions as a rule proceeded precisely by building good superstructures on insecure foundations, and that new sciences had to rely on 'groundwork which is intuitional'" (Simmel, "The Problem of Sociology," translated by Kurt H. Wolff, in Wolff 1959: 326).

5. This point was not lost on Emile Durkheim, who reviewed Small's translation in Volume 1 of the *Anneé Sociologique*, writing:

> Ce n'est pas à dire que le rapport de subordination doive, ou même puisse disparaître; car il est essentiel à la constitution des sociétés: il perd seulement et on peut espérer qu'il perdra de plus en plus ce qu'il peut avoir d'humiliant pour les inférieurs, puisque la supériorité s'abstrait en quelque sorte de la personnalité à laquelle elle était originairement liée. (Durkheim 1897: 155)

6. This statement comes from an advertisement for the *American Journal of Sociology*, which was printed in its first volume and is derived from Small's letter of 25 April 1895 to Chicago's President Harper (see Dibble 1975: 163–68, esp. 165).

7. Or even at the British Museum, where one researcher found the pages of Simmel's *Einleitung in die Moralwissenschaften* (1892) uncut as late as the 1970s (Laurence 1975: 36). The pages are now (1993) cut and professionally preserved.

8. Note the disdain for abstraction and cultural bias in J. M. Robertson's (1909: 299) otherwise favorable review of Simmel's *Die Probleme der Geschichtsphilosophie* (3rd ed., 1907):

> And one cannot but think, once more, that such conclusions [about the inadequacy of strictly empiricist approaches to historical knowledge], which emerge philosophically though not obviously from Dr. Simmel's analysis, might have been more easily reached by way of a concrete handling of historical problems than by a series of circular excursions in the hungry hunting-ground of "Erkenntnistheorie."

9. Information contained in a letter from Howard Woodhead, a student of Small's studying at Berlin, to Small, 6 April 1904 (Albion W. Small Papers, Box 1, University of Chicago). This letter is now published, with an Introduction by Donald N. Levine (1993). In his opinion, Simmel may have been echoing a general sentiment in Germany of the time, as is suggested by Münsterberg's report of having read during his 1903 visit to Germany a long editorial in some newspapers referring to the Congress as a "scholarly Barnum circus" (cited in Coats 1961: 412).

10. Spykman's *Social Theory of Georg Simmel* was a Ph.D. dissertation (1923) written under Frederick J. Teggart, of the University of California,

Berkeley's "Department of Social Institutions." After publishing the dissertation in 1925, and presenting a Simmelian paper on "A Social Philosophy of the City" at an American Sociological Society meeting, later published in the *AJS* (Spykman 1926), Spykman accepted a position at Yale University, where he stayed for the remainder of his career. There, he turned his attention away from Simmel and toward geopolitics (e.g., Spykman 1942), a major interest of Teggart, his Berkeley mentor. The shifting fortunes of Spykman's book on Simmel—from "very much in vogue as something to read" in the 1920s to nearly "completely forgotten" (Hughes 1971)—parallel Spykman's academic shift from sociology to international relations, and are also a result of his premature death in 1943.

11. Lecture Notes on "Interaction," Robert E. Park Papers, Box 5, University of Chicago. These lecture notes, written sometime after 1915, record Simmel's essay in its French title, "L'influence du nombre des unités sociales sur les caractères des sociétés," as published in the transactions of the first congress of the International Institute of Sociology (Simmel 1895). That he cited the French version and not Small's English translation in volume 8 of the *AJS* (1902–1903) suggests that Park was not at this time closely familiar with Small's translations, at least not until later when he came to prepare the selections for *Introduction*.

12. A reviewer has commented that Simmel's own ethical preferences emphasize individual autonomy. While this is true, what is of interest here is the question of Park's, and Small's, apparent decision to underscore not an ethics of individuality but of reciprocity and mutual dependence.

13. Burgess singles out Simmel's essay on super- and subordination as important to the theme of accommodation in his encyclopedia article on the term (Burgess 1930: 403). One of the *Introduction*'s "questions for discussion" reads: "What do you think Simmel means by the term accommodation?" (Park and Burgess 1969 [1921]: 733).

14. Small did not precisely translate the title of Simmel's essay, "*Überordnung und Unterordnung*." He defended his translation of *Überordnung* as "superiority" instead of "superordination," the precise rendering, on the grounds that his choice was "on the whole preferable" (Simmel 1896: 167; translator's note). In the *Introduction*, Park changed the translation to its precise rendering, and in the process signaled his egalitarian convictions.

15. Consider the two leading Columbia sociologists, Franklin H. Giddings and Robert M. MacIver. The former showed little interest in Simmel's work, despite attempts by Small (1902: 559) and Vincent (1896: 487) to draw connections between their work. The latter considered Simmel's *Soziologie* "remarkable" (MacIver 1928: 63, note), but he gave it only modest attention in his early textbook of sociology (MacIver 1937) and none in his later work. Howard Brown Woolston, a Ph.D. (1909) under Giddings, did study with Simmel during a year (1902–1903) abroad. But Woolston made his career at the University of Washington, not Columbia.

16. Information from an interview with Kurt H. Wolff, 7 March 1993, Newton, Massachusetts. A letter and corresponding memo from Hughes to Jerry Kaplan, dated 17 October 1947, systematically compared the contents of *Soziologie* with the Simmel translations in *AJS* (Everett C. Hughes Papers, Box 4, University of Chicago).

17. Others have noted an intellectual affinity between Simmel and Hughes. Coser's reflections on hearing Hughes lecture in Chicago in 1948, for example, record a similarity in their style of delivery:

> Somewhat like Georg Simmel, [Hughes] was apt to move from one subject to the next by what seemed free association, he moved where the spirit dictated, starting to talk, say, about multiethnic contacts only to move after a minute or two to a story about one of his Ohio ancestors, to an account of some experience of Robert Park when working with Booker T. Washington. He moved from large events to seemingly small matters and back again—all in a very few minutes. (Coser 1994: 7–8)

18. Hannah Arendt provides a contemporary account of the situation in this excerpt from her letter to Karl Jaspers in 1949:

> The Red hunt is going full steam. . . . The consequence is that faculty colleagues don't speak openly anymore, particularly at the small, state-supported colleges; and the general fear that at first held sway only in Washington among civil servants now lies like a poisonous cloud over the intellectual life of the whole country. (Arendt and Jaspers 1992 [1949]: 137)

Compare Arendt's account with the recollections of Joseph Gusfield, who was resident at the University of Chicago from 1947–1950:

> Unlike law school . . . in the sociology department there was a greater sense of intellectual and social play. We lived in the Hyde Park area near the university. Graduate-student life was a round of parties, study, and endlessly flamboyant talk. The faculty and classes were its accompaniment as well as its catalyst, but *the talk was where the action was*. (Gusfield 1990: 114; emphasis added)

19. It may be significant to note in this connection that Erving Goffman, who was one of Hughes's students during these years, expressed both a deep cynicism about human affairs and a preference for the small in his first publications (Goffman 1952; 1956).

Chapter 2

1. Consider the two recent major studies of Goffman: Burns (1992) and Manning (1992). Doyle is not listed in the index to either book. Park is

listed twice in Burns, not at all in Manning. Hughes is given attention in both studies, but an adequate study of Hughes and Goffman has yet to be published.

2. Goffman attended the University of Chicago from 1945 to 1953, when he took his Ph.D. From 1954 to 1957, he conducted field research for his book *Asylums* (1961a).

3. This brief review examines the citations in Goffman's writings, not citations of Goffman's work by others. For a discussion of the latter, see Oromaner (1980).

4. This paragraph draws on information presented in the previous chapter.

5. In his essay "On Presumption," Montaigne writes: "We are nothing but ceremony; ceremony carries us away, and we leave the substance of things" (Montaigne 1947 [1580]: 120).

6. In an article that previews the book, Doyle alludes to the use of "etiquette as mask" (Doyle 1971 [1936]: 121), but it is mentioned only in passing and is overshadowed by the Spencerian view of etiquette as control.

7. Doyle and Hughes were intimate acquaintances, sharing religion, schooling, and generational experiences. Hughes's father was a Methodist minister; Doyle himself was an ordained minister and later Bishop of the Christian Methodist Episcopal Church. Both Hughes (in 1918) and Doyle (in 1921) were graduates of Ohio Wesleyan Methodist College; and they were together graduate students at the University of Chicago, completing their Ph.D. degrees (Hughes 1928, Doyle 1934) under Robert E. Park. The Hughes–Doyle correspondence in the Everett C. Hughes Papers (Box 20, folder 10) of the University of Chicago Library reveals that the bonds formed during their graduate school years were followed by infrequent but close contact in later years.

8. Hughes (1950: xi) makes the point that an interactionist interpretation of accommodation was consistent with Park's own writings.

9. Is this last example of the intellectual entrepreneur self-referential? Was Goffman sending a message to his teachers that he was playing at their game, adopting their intellectual tools but preserving his freedom? These are interesting questions to which we may never know the answers. See Winkin (1988; 1996) for a view of Goffman's work as fully self-referential or autobiographical.

10. Goffman was, of course, well versed in the literature of Chicago sociology. This familiarity extended to Doyle's study of southern etiquette, which he references in his dissertation (Goffman 1953a: 223). This reference, however, is not to Doyle's discussion of role play, but to examples

from the Old South illustrating Goffman's notion of the "non-person." But, I am not arguing that Goffman was "influenced" by Doyle; rather, I take the position that Park's framework created a theoretical opening, as it were, for the type of conceptual development advanced independently by both Doyle and Goffman. My thanks to Andrew Travers for drawing my attention to the Doyle reference in Goffman's dissertation. In a recent paper, Travers (1996) explores Goffman's notion of the "non-person" and its sources.

11. In an interview with Verhoeven (1993: 318, 324), Goffman twice identifies his work as traditionally functionalist. The conventional understanding of interactionist and functional sociology as alternative and competing schools of thought has obscured the intellectual interchange between the two approaches. In addition to Hughes and Goffman, Shibutani (1962) exploited useful lines of convergence. Whether these attempts were made out of strength or weakness, and whether there were corresponding efforts from the other direction, are interesting research questions.

CHAPTER 3

1. I refer throughout to the pagination of the original drafted chapter, which is located in the Parsons Papers of the Harvard University Archives (Parsons 1936). The chapter bears the title, "*Georg Simmel* and *Ferdinand Toennies*: Social Relationships and the Elements of Action." The part of the chapter devoted to Toennies was included in *Structure of Social Action* as "A Note on *Gemeinschaft* and *Gesellschaft*" (Parsons 1968 [1937]: 686–94). Since it is the chapter's section on Simmel that was excluded, not the entire chapter, I will refer to the manuscript as "the section on Simmel." The full chapter is now published in the *Simmel Newsletter* (Vol. 4, No. 1, 1994), among other places.

2. Both outlines are located in the Parsons Papers, MSSA, Box 3.

3. Levine had earlier dismissed Parsons's own explanation of his decision on the grounds that it implies that he was acting in a "self-serving manner," and that Parsons had elsewhere eschewed such explanations of intellectual matters as invalid (Levine 1980 [1957]: xxxi). He now grants the validity of considering intellectual competition a factor in explaining Parsons's decision to exclude the section on Simmel from *Structure* (Levine 1991).

4. The Department of Sociology Minutes for 15 April 1936 record the details of the Becker recommendation. See Sociology, Division and Department of, Minutes, 1931–1945, UA V.801–5, in the Harvard University Archives.

CHAPTER 4

1. As Arnold Simmel, Georg's grandson, surmises, "his [Naegele's] contact with us must have pricked his interest in Simmel, and finding him congenial to his way of thinking, he threw himself into reading Simmel—with energy, concentration, understanding and learning" (A. Simmel 1981).

2. My request for information on Naegele in the American Sociological Association's "Footnotes" (December 1980) yielded mainly letters of admiration for Naegele the man.

3. In a revealing letter to Naegele, Parsons commented on a draft of his collaborator's introductory essay for *Theories of Society*. He disapproved of Naegele's "extensive attention to Durkheim and Simmel, particularly the latter," and suggested he reduce the discussion of these figures,"or at least balance them with more extensive discussions" of Weber and Freud (Parsons 1958: 1).

4. Information from an interview with Drs. Elaine and John Cumming, 21 January 1981.

CHAPTER 5

1. For a complete analysis of Merton's Simmel reception in the mid-1950s, see Jaworski (1989).

2. This information is based on an interview I conducted with Professor Merton in his office at the Russell Sage Foundation, 17 February, 1988.

3. Information from Merton interview, 17 February, 1988.

4. Merton mentions his study, with Paul F. Lazarfeld (1954), of friendship as bearing on the concept of observability (Merton 1957: 321). Also, in *The Student Physician*, reference is made to the term in a discussion of the difference between being monitored in medical school and the absence of such monitoring in private practice (Merton et al. 1957). See also, Merton (1976: 71).

5. This terminological confusion extends to subsequent discussions and applications of Merton's terms. Sztompka (1986) clearly distinquishes between property of social position and property of observable (the above discussion follows his discriminating analysis). However, he does not reveal the ambiguity of the original and he himself continues the confusion by assigning the term "observability" to that which Merton explicitly calls "visibility" (Sztompka 1986: 170; Merton 1957: 350). Cole and Cole (1968) employ the terms "visibility" and "awareness." The latter term, they write, "we substitute . . . for 'observability.'" But since Merton does not use "observability" in a consistent way it is not at all clear what this statement means.

Rose Coser (1961) gains consistency by writing only of "observability." Lewis A. Coser (1975: 97), following Merton, referred to "visibility or observability." And Peter Blau (1975: 137), perhaps recognizing the conceptual difference at stake, referred to Merton's discussion of "visibility and observability."

6. It is perhaps significant to report in this connection that Merton's book, *On the Shoulders of Giants*, was written in 1958, a year after the publication of the second edition of STSS containing the "Continuities" chapter. The book was not published until 1965, however. See Merton (1985: 485).

CHAPTER 6

1. This phrase was borrowed from Jürgen Habermas (1982: 222) and was brought to my attention by Bernstein (1983: 227).

2. I used information from the following sources constructing this biographical sketch and in writing this chapter: brief biographies of Coser in *Contemporary Authors* (1963: 207) and in Wald (1987: 323–24); Coser's own autobiographical writings (Rosenberg 1984; Coser 1988a, 1988b); and two interview with Professor Coser, one in Baltimore on 18 March 1989 and the other in Cambridge on 2 October 1989.

3. Many other scholars could have been cited as well. The justification for mentioning these writers is that Coser cites all of them in his dissertation (e.g., Coser 1954: 133, note 272). For a much longer list of names and writings, along with an attempt to defend Mayo against the criticisms contained in those writings, see Landsberger (1958: Ch. 3).

That Coser's dissertation was a part of this critical wave of thought has been hidden from view, in part, because the published version, *The Functions of Social Conflict*, omits the portion of the study containing Coser's contributions to the literature. Coser discusses briefly the circumstances surrounding the publication of *Functions*, and the decision to include only a summary of the part that concerns us here, in (Rosenberg 1984: 44).

4. Coser often quoted the famous line from Marx's "Introduction to the Critique of Hegel's Philosophy of Right": "the demand to abandon illusions about their condition is a demand to abandon a condition which requires illusion," in Easton and Guddat (1967: 250). See, for example, Coser (1954: 224).

5. I take this argument about the strategic uses of social theory from Buxton (1985), who applies it to Talcott Parsons.

CHAPTER 7

1. The original manuscript suffers from many defects, including repetition, incompleteness, deleted sections, inconsistent verb tense and other

grammatical problems. Turning the manuscript into a coherent and readable essay was a challenge and required some modification of the original. When forced to choose between clarity of expression and fidelity to the original, I chose the former. I have altered passages in light of the author's suggested revisions (found in the marginalia) as well as in the interest of style and consistency. For example, the manuscript begins with some occasional remarks and biographical reflections, which for the purpose of coherence are not included here. Finally, all section headings and notes have been added by the editor. The title is the author's.

2. In additional to these observations on Simmel, Salomon also contributed several paragraphs to the volume of reminiscences on Simmel published on the centenary of his birth: Kurt Gassen and Michael Landmann, editors, *Buch des Dankes an Georg Simmel* (Berlin: Dunker & Humblot, 1958). My thanks to Professor Guy Oakes for this reference.

3. *Uns kan keener.* Lewis A. Coser, a Berlin native, has suggested the following translation of this curious phrase: "Nobody can impress us—we can rely on our native wit." My thanks to Professor Coser for this contribution.

4. Salomon does not provide a citation for this autobiographical remark.

5. I have been unable to locate a quotation that fits exactly Salomon's statement, but the following passages come close to it: "Schopenhauer . . . is without doubt a greater philosopher than Nietzsche . . . [who] is not challenged by metaphysical questions but moral ones, and he is not looking for the essence of being but for the innate imperatives and for the being of the human soul. . . . [T]he great style of Schopenhauer . . . evolves from his having been attuned not only to the sounds of men and their values, but also to the primeval music of being." Georg Simmel, *Schopenhauer and Nietzsche.* Translated by Helmut Loiskandl, Michael Weinstein, and Deena Weinstein. (Amherst, MA: The University of Massachusetts Press, 1986), p. 13.

6. Wilhelm Dilthey, *Introduction to the Human Sciences*, edited and introduced by Rudolf A. Makkreel and Frithjof Rodi. (Princeton: Princeton University Press, 1989), pp. 497–98.

7. For a discussion of Lask's (1875–1915) philosophy in relation to the methodology of Max Weber, see Guy Oakes, "Weber and the Southwest German School: The Genesis of the Concept of the Historical Individual." In *Max Weber and His Contemporaries*, edited by Wolfgang J. Mommsen and Jurgen Osterhammel. (London: Allen & Unwin 1987), pp. 434–46.

8. An English translation of this letter can be found in *Georg Simmel*, edited by Lewis A. Coser. (Englewood Cliffs, NJ: Prentice-Hall, 1965), pp. 37–39.

9. The Kracauer reference undoubtedly alludes to Siegfried Kracauer's study of white-collar employees in Berlin, *Die Angestellten*, in his *Schriften*,

1 (Frankfurt: Suhrkamp, 1971). As was mentioned in the Introduction, Kracauer was in the audience during the reading and discussion of Salomon's paper.

10. Salomon incorrectly identified Braunau as being in the Sudetenland. It is in fact on the Inn River, the boundary between Austria and German. My thanks to Professor Gerd Schroeter, Lakehead University, for this correction.

11. See Goethe's *Faust*, Part II, Act IV, line 10176.

12. *Quand meme* means literally, "nevertheless" or "all the same," a scholar's retort to life's limitations.

13. José Ortega y Gasset, "In Search of Goethe from Within." *Partisan Review* 16 (December 1949), pp. 1163–88, reference at 1166.

14. This phrase resists easy English translation, but might be rendered as "Refined sadness, never ridiculous." Salomon's phrase introduces an implied comparison of Simmel's writings with *la Préciosité*, a French cultured style of the seventeenth century involving refined, even exaggerated, manners and florid writing. Molière satirized its excesses in *Les Précieuses Ridicules* (1659). Thanks to my colleague, Dr. Richard Kopp, for this information.

15. Georg Simmel, *The Philosophy of Money*, edited by David Frisby, translated by Tom Bottomore and David Frisby from a first draft by Kaethe Mengelberg, 2nd enlarged ed. (NY: Routledge, 1990), pp. 223–25.

16. Georg Simmel, *Soziologie*. Chapter VIII, "Der selbsterhaltung der Gruppe." (Leipzig: Dunker & Humblot, 1908), pp. 494–613.

17. I have modified somewhat Salomon's translation from Simmel's *Soziologie*, p. 599.

18. Simmel, *Soziologie*, Chapter IX, "Der Raum und die Raumlichen Ordnungen der Gesellschaft," pp. 614–708.

19. This reference is to "L'Illustre Gaudissart," a character from Balzac who illustrates a new social type emerging along with the transformations in capitalism (see Pugh 1974). My thanks to Professor Patrick Watier, Universite de Sciences Humaines de Strasbourg, for this information.

20. Alfred Schutz, "The Stranger: An Essay in Social Psychology." In his *Collected Papers*, Vol. II, edited and introduced by Arvid Broderson. (The Hague: Martinus Nijhoff, 1971), pp. 91–105.

21. Gertrud Kantorowicz, editor, *Fragmente und Aufsätze aus dem Nachlass und Veröffentlichungen der letzen Jahre* (Munich: Drei-Masken-Verlag, 1923), p. 17.

22. A reference, presumably, to the story of Shylock in Shakespeare's *The Merchant of Venice*.

23. That is, philosophy is necessary to live, not as a way of making a living.

24. *Totum se dedit*, that is, he was wholly absorbed in (or dedicated to) his work. Karl Mannheim reportedly said this about himself to Salomon. See Albert Salomon, "Karl Mannheim, 1893–1947." *Social Research* 14 (September 1947), p. 351.

25. See Charles Louis de Secondat, Baron de Montesquieu, T*he Spirit of the Laws*, Book XXV, Chapter 13.

26. In the original manuscript, several paragraphs follow which address earlier points. These paragraphs have been incorporated into the body of the text at appropriate places.

CHAPTER 8

1. These papers are now collected and published in *Postmodern(ized) Simmel*, where the authors respond briefly to my critique of their work (Weinstein and Weinstein 1993: 225, note 4). The validity of my critique and of their response to it must be decided by others.

REFERENCES

ABBREVIATIONS

PP	Parsons Papers, Harvard University Archives
CM 1930s–1960s	Course materials (PP)
CRP 1923–1940	Correspondence and related papers (PP)
CRP 1930–1959	Correspondence and related papers (PP)
CRP 1953–1955	Correspondence and related papers (PP)
CRP 1965–1979	Correspondence and related papers (PP)
LNA 1929–1978	Lecture notes and addresses (PP)
MBMW n.d.	Manuscript of books and major theoretical works (PP)
MSSA n.d.	Manuscript of *Structure of Social Action* and other works (PP)
UM 1929–1967	Unpublished manuscripts (PP)

Abel, Theodore. 1929. *Systematic Sociology in Germany.* New York: Columbia University Press.

Alexander, Jeffrey. 1979. Letter to Talcott Parsons, 9 January. PP, CRP 1965–1979, Box 1.

Arendt, Hannah and Karl Jaspers. 1992. *Correspondence 1926–1969*, edited by Lotte Kohler and Hans Saner; translated by Robert and Rita Kimber. New York: Harcourt Brace Jovanovich.

Adams, Henry. 1961 [1918]. *The Education of Henry Adams.* Boston: Houghton Mifflin.

Ahlstrom, Sydney E. 1975. *A Religious History of the American People.* Vol. 2. Garden City, NY: Doubleday.

Attewell, Paul. 1984. *Radical Political Economy since the Sixties.* New Brunswick, NJ: Rutgers University Press.

Baldwin, James Mark, editor. 1901–1905. *Dictionary of Philosophy and Psychology.* New York: Macmillan.

Baldwin, James Mark. 1902. *Development and Evolution*. New York: Macmillan.

Baudelaire, Charles. 1964. *The Painter of Modern Life and Other Essays*. Oxford: Phaidon.

Bell, Daniel. 1947. "Adjusting Men to Machines: Social Scientists Explore the World of the Factory." *Commentary* 3: 79–88.

Bell, Daniel. 1958. Letter to Kaspar Naegele. Naegele Papers.

Bell, Wendell and Jeffrey K. Olick. 1989. "An Epistemology for the Futures Field," *Futures* (April): 115–35.

Bendix, Reinhard. 1947. "Bureaucracy: The Problem and its Setting." *American Sociological Review* 12: 493–507.

Bendix, Reinhard. 1970. *Embattled Reason: Essays on Social Knowledge*. New York: Oxford University Press.

Bendix, Reinhard and Lloyd H. Fisher. 1949. "The Perspectives of Elton Mayo." *The Review of Economics and Statistics* 31: 312–19.

Bendix, Reinhard and Bennett Berger. 1959. "Images of Society and Problems of Concept Formation in Sociology." Pp. 92–118 in *Symposium on Sociological Theory*, edited by Llewellyn Gross. Evanston, IL: Row, Peterson and Co.

Benjamin, Walter. 1973. *Charles Baudelaire: A Lyric Poet in the Era of High Capitalism*. London: New Left Books.

Berger, Morroe, Theodore Abel, and Charles H. Page, eds. 1954. *Freedom and Control in Modern Society*. New York: D. Van Nostrand Company.

Bernert, Chris. 1982. "From Cameralism to Sociology with Albion Small." *Journal of the History of Sociology* 4: 32–63.

Bernstein, Richard J. 1983. *Beyond Objectivism and Relativism: Science, Hermeneutics, And Praxis*. Philadelphia: University of Pennsylvania Press.

Bershady, Harold J. 1973. *Ideology and Social Knowledge*. New York: John Wiley & Sons.

Besnard, Philippe. 1986. "The Americanization of Anomie at Harvard." *Knowledge and Society* 6: 138–47.

Besnard, Philippe. 1987. *L'anomie. Ses usages et ses fonctions dans la discipline sociologique depuis Durkheim*. Paris: Universitaires de France.

Besnard, Philippe. 1988. "The True Nature of Anomie." *Sociological Theory* 6: 91–95.

Bierstedt, Robert. 1981. *American Sociological Theory: A Critical History.* New York: Academic Press.

Blau, Peter M. 1956. *Bureaucracy in Modern Society.* New York: Random House.

Blau, Peter M. 1975. "Structural Constraints of Status Complements." Pp. 117–38 in Lewis Coser, ed. *The Idea of Social Structure.*

Bloom, Harold. 1975. *A Map of Misreading.* New York: Oxford University Press.

Blumer, Herbert. 1947. "Sociological Theory in Industrial Relations." *American Sociological Review* 12: 271–78.

Bovone, Laura. 1993. "Ethics as Etiquette: The Emblematic Contribution of Erving Goffman." *Theory, Culture & Society* 10: 25–39.

Burawoy, Michael. 1982. "The Written and Repressed in Gouldner's Industrial Sociology." *Theory and Society* 11: 831–51.

Burgess, Ernest W. 1930. "Accommodation." Pp. 403–4 in *Encyclopedia of the Social Sciences.* Vol. 1. New York: Macmillan.

Burns, Tom. 1992. *Erving Goffman.* New York: Routledge.

Buxton, William. 1985. *Talcott Parsons and the Capitalist Nation State.* Toronto: University of Toronto Press.

Buxton, William and Stephen P. Turner. 1992. "From Education to Expertise: Sociology as a Profession." Pp. 373–407 in *Sociology and Its Publics: The Forms and Fates of Disciplinary Organization,* edited by Terence C. Halliday and Morris Janowitz. Chicago: University of Chicago Press.

Chriss, James J. 1995. "Some Thoughts on Recent Efforts to Further Systematize Goffman." *Sociological Forum* 10: 177–86.

Coats, A. W. 1961. "American Scholarship Comes of Age: The Louisiana Purchase Exposition 1904." *Journal of the History of Ideas* 22: 404–17.

Cole, Stephen and Jonathan R. Cole. 1968. "Visibility and the Structural Bases of Awareness of Scientific Research." *American Sociological Review* 33: 397–413.

Collins, Randall. 1981 [1979]. "Three Stages of Erving Goffman." In his *Sociology Since Midcentury.* New York: Academic Press.

Contemporary Authors. 1963. "Coser, Lewis A." 207.

Coser, Lewis A. 1954. "Toward a Sociology of Social Conflict." Ph.D. diss. Columbia University.

Coser, Lewis A. 1956a. *The Functions of Social Conflict.* Glencoe, Illinois: The Free Press.

Coser, Lewis A. 1956b. "What Shall We Do?" *Dissent* 3: 156–65.

Coser, Lewis A., ed. 1965. *Georg Simmel.* Englewood Cliffs, NJ: Prentice-Hall.

Coser, Lewis A., ed. 1975. *The Idea of Social Structure: Papers in Honor of Robert K. Merton.* New York: Harcourt Brace Jovanovich.

Coser, Lewis A. 1988a. *A Handful of Thistles: Collected Papers in Moral Conviction.* New Brunswick, NJ: Transaction.

Coser, Lewis A. 1988b. "Notes on a Double Career." Pp. 65–70 in *Sociological Lives,* edited by Matilda White Riley. Newbury Park, CA: Sage.

Coser, Lewis A., ed. 1994. *Everett C. Hughes: Work, Race and the Sociological Imagination.* Chicago: University of Chicago Press.

Coser, Rose Laub. 1961. "Insulation from Observability and Types of Social Conformity." *American Sociological Review* 26: 843–53.

Derrida, Jacques. 1974. *Of Grammatology.* Translated by G. C. Spivak. Baltimore: Johns Hopkins University Press.

Dibble, Vernon K. 1975. *The Legacy of Albion Small.* Chicago: University of Chicago Press.

Doyle, Bertram W. 1937. *The Etiquette of Race Relations in the South: A Study in Social Control.* Chicago: University of Chicago Press.

Doyle, Bertram W. 1971 [1936]. "The Etiquette of Race Relations—Past, Present, and Future." Pp. 107–23 in *The Black Sociologists: The First Half Century,* edited by John H. Bracey, Jr., August Meier, and Elliott Rudwick. Belmont, CA: Wadsworth.

Durkheim, Emile. 1897. Review of "Superiority and Subordination as a Subject-Matter of Sociology," by Georg Simmel. *L' Année Sociologique* 1: 152–55.

Durkheim, Emile and Paul Fauconnet. 1904. "Sociology and the Social Sciences." *Sociological Papers* 1: 258–80.

Durkheim, Emile, et. al. 1960. *Essays on Sociology and Philosophy.* Edited by Kurt H. Wolff. New York: Harper & Row.

Easton, Loyd D. and Kurt H. Guddat, eds. 1967. *Writings of the Young Marx on Philosophy and Society.* New York: Anchor/Doubleday.

Franklin, Fabian. 1910. *The Life of Daniel Coit Gilman.* New York: Dodd, Mead.

Fredrickson, George M. 1971. *The Black Image in the White Mind: The Debate on Afro-American Character and Destiny, 1817–1914*. New York: Harper & Row.

Freund, Peter E. S. 1982. *The Civilized Body: Social Domination, Control and Health*. Philadelphia: Temple University Press.

Frisby, David. 1981. *Sociological Impressionism: A Reassessment of Georg Simmel's Social Theory*. London: Heinemann.

Frisby, David. 1985. "Georg Simmel, First Sociologist of Modernity." *Theory, Culture & Society* 2: 49–67.

Frisby, David. 1986. *Fragments of Modernity: Theories of Modernity in the Work of Simmel, Kracauer, and Benjamin*. Cambridge: MIT Press.

Frisby, David. 1991a. "Bibliographical Note on Simmel's Works in Translation." *Theory, Culture & Society* 8: 235–41.

Frisby, David. 1991b. "The Aesthetics of Modern Life: Simmel's Interpretation." *Theory, Culture & Society* 8: 73–93.

Frisby, David. 1992. *Simmel and Since: Essays on Georg Simmel's Social Theory*. London: Routledge.

Gadamer, Hans-Georg. 1975 [1965]. *Truth and Method*. New York: Seabury.

Gassen, Kurt. 1959. "Bibliography of Writings on Georg Simmel." Pp. 357–75 in *Georg Simmel: 1858–1918*, edited by Kurt H. Wolff. Columbus: The Ohio State University Press.

Gephardt, Werner. 1982. "Soziologie im Aufbruch: Zur Wechselwirkung von Durkheim, Schäffle, Toennies und Simmel." *Koelner Zeitschrift für Soziologie* 34: 1–25.

Gerth, Hans H. and C. Wright Mills. 1958 [1946]. "Preface." In *From Max Weber: Essays in Sociology*, by Max Weber. Translated, edited, and with an Introduction by Hans H. Gerth and C. Wright Mills. New York: Oxford University Press.

Goffman, Erving. 1951. "Symbols of Class Status." *British Journal of Sociology* 2:294–304.

Goffman, Erving. 1952. "On Cooling the Mark Out: Some Aspects of Adaptation to Failure." *Psychiatry* 15 (November): 451–63.

Goffman, Erving. 1953a. "Communication Conduct in an Island Community." Unpublished Ph.D. dissertation, University of Chicago.

Goffman, Erving. 1953b. "The Service Station Dealer: The Man and His Work." Chicago: Social Research.

142   REFERENCES

Goffman, Erving. 1956. *The Presentation of Self in Everyday Life.* University of Edinburgh Social Sciences Research Centre, Monograph No. 2.

Goffman, Erving. 1959. *Presentation of Self in Everyday Life.* New York: Doubleday.

Goffman, Erving. 1961a. *Asylums: Essays on the Social Situation of Mental Patients and Other Inmates.* New York: Doubleday.

Goffman, Erving. 1961b. *Encounters: Two Studies in the Sociology of Interaction.* New York: Bobbs-Merrill.

Goffman, Erving. 1967 [1955]. "On Face Work." In his *Interaction Ritual.* New York: Doubleday.

Goffman, Erving. 1971. *Relations in Public.* New York: Basic.

Goffman, Erving. 1974. *Frame Analysis.* New York: Harper & Row.

Goffman, Erving. 1981. "A Reply to Denzin and Keller." *Contemporary Sociology* 10: 60–68.

Gouldner, Alvin W. 1954. *Patterns of Industrial Bureaucracy.* Glencoe, IL: The Free Press.

Gouldner, Alvin W.. 1955. "Metaphysical Pathos and the Theory of Bureaucracy." *American Political Science Review* 49: 496–507.

Greek, Cecil. 1992. *The Religious Roots of American Sociology.* New York: Garland.

Grimshaw, Allen D. 1959. "Lawlessness and Violence in America and Their Special Manifestations in Changing Negro-White Relationships." *The Journal of Negro History* 44: 52–72.

Gusfield, Joseph. 1990. "My Life and Soft Times." Pp. 104–29 in *Authors of Their Own Lives,* edited by Bennett M. Berger. Berkeley: University of California Press.

Habermas, Jürgen. 1982. "A Reply to My Critics." Pp. 263–69 in *Habermas: Critical Debates,* edited by John B. Thompson and David Held. Cambridge, MA: M.I.T. Press.

Halliday, Terrence C. and Morris Janowitz, eds. 1992. *Sociology and Its Publics: The Forms and Fates of Disciplinary Organization.* Chicago: University of Chicago Press.

Harsha, E. Houston. 1952 [1949]. "Illinois: The Broyles Commission." Pp. 54–139 in *The States and Subversion,* edited by Walter Gellhorn. Ithaca, NY: Cornell University Press.

Hawkins, Hugh. 1960. *Pioneer: A History of the Johns Hopkins University, 1874–1889.* Ithaca, New York: Cornell University Press.

Hayner, Norman. n.d. "Robert E. Park: Recollections, Insights, Evaluation." Robert E. Park Papers, Box 7, University of Chicago.

Helmes-Hayes, Rick. 1994. "'I Have Trod the Ecological Path': Everett Hughes' Interpretive Institutional Ecology." Unpublished manuscript.

Herbst, Jurgen. 1965. *The German Historical School in American Scholarship.* Ithaca, NY: Cornell University Press.

Hettlage, Robert and Karl Lenz, eds. 1991. *Erving Goffman-ein soziologischer Klasssiker der zweiten Generation.* Bern and Stutgart: Paul Haupt.

Hinkle, Gisela J. 1986. "The Americanization of Max Weber." *Current Perspectives in Social Theory* 7: 87–104.

Hofstadter, Richard. 1955. *Social Darwinism in American Thought.* Boston: Beacon.

Hollinger, David A. 1991. "Justification by Verification: The Scientific Challenge to the Moral Authority of Christianity in Modern America." Pp. 116–35 in *Religion and Twentieth Century American Intellectual Life*, edited by Michael Lacey. New York: Cambridge University Press.

Hughes, Everett C. 1939. "Institutions" in *Principles of Sociology*, edited by Alfred McClung Lee. New York: Barnes & Noble.

Hughes, Everett C. 1945. "Dilemmas and Contradictions in Status." *American Journal of Sociology* 50: 353–59.

Hughes, Everett C. 1947. Letter to Jerry Kaplan, 17 October, Everett C. Hughes Papers, Box 4, University of Chicago.

Hughes, Everett C. 1950. "Preface" to *Race and Culture*, by Robert E. Park. New York: Free Press.

Hughes, Everett C. 1952 [1947]. "Principle and Rationalization in Race Relations." In his *Where People Meet* (with Helen MacGill Hughes). New York: Free Press.

Hughes, Everett C. 1953. Untitled History of the Sociology Department of the University of Chicago, Everett C. Hughes Papers, Box 7, University of Chicago.

Hughes, Everett C. 1954a. Letter to Kurt H. Wolff, 11 June, Everett C. Hughes Papers, Box 12a, University of Chicago.

Hughes, Everett C. 1954b. Letter to Jerry Kaplan, Kurt H. Wolff, and Reinhard Bendix, June 19, Everett C. Hughes Papers, Box 12a, University of Chicago.

Hughes, Everett C. 1955. "Foreword." Pp. 7–9 in Georg Simmel, *Conflict and the Web of Group Affiliations*. Translated by Kurt H. Wolff and Reinhard Bendix. New York: Free Press.

Hughes, Everett C. 1958 [1952]. "Cycles, Turning Points and Careers." Chapter 1 in his *Men and Their Work*. Glencoe, IL: The Free Press.

Hughes, Everett C. 1963 [1943]. *French Canada in Transition*. Chicago: University of Chicago Press.

Hughes, Everett C. 1964. "Robert E. Park." *New Society* (13 December): 18–19.

Hughes, Everett C. 1965. "A Note on Georg Simmel." *Social Problems* 13: 117–18.

Hughes, Everett C. 1970. Letter to Donald N. Levine, 11–12 March, Everett C. Hughes Papers, Box 7, University of Chicago.

Hughes, Everett C. 1971 [1928]. "Personality Types and the Division of Labor." Chapter 33 in his *The Sociological Eye: Selected Papers*. Chicago: Aldine.

Hughes, Everett C. 1971. Letter to Donald N. Levine, 8 October, Everett C. Hughes Papers, Box 26, University of Chicago.

Jacoby, Russell. 1987. *The Last Intellectuals: American Culture in the Age of Academe*. New York: Basic.

Jamieson, Stuart. 1965. "Portrait of a Scholar." *The Canadian Scholar* 45 (April).

Janowitz, Morris. 1965. Review of Ralph Elison, *Shadow and Act. American Journal of Sociology* 70: 732–734.

Jaworski, Gary Dean. 1983. "Simmel and the *Année*." *Journal of the History of Sociology* 5: 28–41.

Jaworski, Gary Dean. 1989. "The Fate of Georg Simmel in Functionalist Sociology, 1937–1961." Unpublished Ph.D. dissertation, New School For Social Research.

Jaworski, Gary Dean. 1990. "Robert K. Merton's Extension of Simmel's *Übersehbar*." *Sociological Theory* 8: 99–105.

Jaworski, Gary Dean. 1991. "The Historical and Contemporary Importance of Coser's *Functions*." *Sociological Theory* 9: 116–23.

Johnson, Alvin S. 1952. *Pioneer's Progress: An Autobiography*. New York: Viking.

Kalberg, Stephen. 1993. "Salomon's Interpretation of Max Weber." *International Journal of Politics, Culture and Society* 6 (Summer): 585–94.

Kennedy, Paul M. 1980. *The Rise of the Anglo-German Antagonism, 1860–1914*. London: Allen and Unwin.

Kluckhohn, Clyde, et al. 1951. "Values and Value-Orientations in the Theory of Action." Pp. 388–433 in *Toward a General Theory of Action*, edited by Talcott Parsons and Edward Shils. New York: Harper.

Koelb, Clayton. 1990. "Introduction: So What's the Story?" Pp. 1–18 in *Nietzsche as Postmodernist: Essays Pro and Contra*, edited by C. Koelb. New York: SUNY Press.

König, René. 1968. "Wiese, Leopold von." Pp. 547–49 in *International Encyclopedia of the Social Sciences*. Vol. 16. New York: Macmillan and the Free Press.

Landsberger, Henry A. 1958. *Hawthorne Revisited*. Ithaca, NY: Cornell University Press.

Laurence, Alfred E. 1975. "Georg Simmel: Triumph and Tragedy." *International Journal of Contemporary Sociology* 12: 28–48.

Levine, Donald N. 1957. "Simmel and Parsons: Two Approaches to the Study of Society." Ph.D. diss., University of Chicago.

Levine, Donald N. 1971. "Introduction." Pp. ix–lxv in *Georg Simmel: On Individuality and Social Forms*. Chicago: University of Chicago Press.

Levine, Donald N. 1972. "Note on *The Crowd and the Public*," Pp. xxvii–xxxii in Robert E. Park, *The Crowd and the Public and Other Essays*. Translated by Charlotte Elsner. Edited and with an Introduction by Henry Elsner, Jr. Chicago: University of Chicago Press.

Levine, Donald N. 1980 [1957]. "Introduction to the Arno Press Edition." *Simmel and Parsons: Two Approaches to the Study of Society*. New York: Arno Press.

Levine, Donald N. 1985. *The Flight from Ambiguity: Essays in Social and Cultural Theory*. Chicago: University of Chicago Press.

Levine, Donald N. 1989. "Simmel Studies in Europe." *Perspectives* (The ASA Theory Section Newsletter) 12: 4.

Levine, Donald N. 1991. "Simmel and Parsons Reconsidered." *American Journal of Sociology* 96: 1097–1116.

Levine, Donald N. 1993. "Howard Woodhead—An American Correspondent on Simmel." *Simmel Newsletter* 3 (Summer): 74–78.

Levine, Donald N., Ellwood B. Carter, and Eleanor Miller Gorman. 1976. "Simmel's Influence on American Sociology." *American Journal of Sociology* 81: 813–45; 1112–32.

Lévi-Strauss, Claude. 1966. *The Savage Mind.* Chicago: University of Chicago Press.

Liebersohn, Harry. 1982. "Leopold von Wiese and the Ambivalence of Functionalist Sociology." *European Journal of Sociology* 23:123–49.

Liebersohn, Harry. 1988. *Fate and Utopia in German Sociology, 1870–1923.* Cambridge: MIT Press.

Lyman, Stanford M. 1972. *The Black American in Sociological Thought.* NY: Putnam's.

Lyman, Stanford M. 1992. *Militarism, Imperialism, and Racial Accommodation: An Analysis and Interpretation of the Early Writings of Robert E. Park.* Fayetteville: University of Arkansas Press.

Lynd, Robert S. 1946. *Knowledge for What?* Princeton: Princeton University Press.

Lyotard, Jean-François. 1984. *The Postmodern Condition: A Report on Knowledge.* Minneapolis: University of Minnesota Press.

Lyotard, Jean-François. 1991. *The Inhuman: Reflections on Time.* Stanford: Stanford University Press.

McKee, James B. 1993. *Sociology and the Race Problem: The Failure of Perspective.* Urbana: University of Illinois Press.

MacCannell, Dean. 1983. "Erving Goffman (1922–1982)." *Semiotica* 45, 1/2: 1–33.

MacIver, Robert M. 1928. *Community: A Sociological Study.* NY: Macmillan.

MacIver, Robert M. 1937. *Society: A Textbook of Sociology.* NY: Farrar & Rinehart.

Mannheim, Karl. 1936. *Ideology and Utopia.* Translated by Louis Wirth and Edward Shils. New York: Harcourt, Brace & World.

Mannheim, Karl. 1982. *Structures of Thinking.* Translated by Jeremy Shapiro and Shierry Weber Nicholsen. Edited and Introduced by David Kettler, Volker Meja and Nico Stehr. New York: Routledge.

Manning, Philip. 1992. *Erving Goffman and Modern Sociology.* Stanford: Stanford University Press.

Martel, Martin U. 1979. "Parsons, Talcott." Pp. 609–30 in *International Encyclopedia of the Social Sciences: Biographical Supplement.* Edited by David Sills. New York: Free Press.

Mayo, Elton. 1933. *The Human Problems of an Industrial Civilization.* New York: Macmillan.

Mayo, Elton. 1946. *The Social Problem of an Industrial Civilization*. Boston: Graduate School of Business Administration, Harvard University.

Merton, Robert K. 1954. "Friendship as a Social Process: A Substantive and Methodological Analysis" (with Paul F. Lazarsfeld). Pp. 18–66 in *Freedom and Control in Modern Society*, edited by Morroe Berger, et. al. New York: D. Van Nostrand.

Merton, Robert K. 1957. *Social Theory and Social Structure*. Revised and enlarged edition. New York: The Free Press.

Merton, Robert K, George G. Reader, Patricia L. Kendell, et al. 1957. *The Student-Physician*. Cambridge: Harvard University Press.

Merton, Robert K. 1965. *On the Shoulders of Giants: A Shandean Postscript*. New York: The Free Press.

Merton, Robert K. 1967. "On the History and Systematics of Sociological Theory." In his *On Theoretical Sociology*. New York: Free Press.

Merton, Robert K. 1973. *The Sociology of Science: Theoretical and Empirical Investigations*. Chicago: University of Chicago Press.

Merton, Robert K. 1976. *Sociological Ambivalence*. New York: The Free Press.

Merton, Robert K. 1980. "Remembering the Young Talcott Parsons." *The American Sociologist* 15: 68–71.

Merton, Robert K. 1985. "George Sarton: Episodic Recollections by an Unruly Apprentice." *ISIS* 76: 470–86.

Mill, John Stuart. 1872. *A System of Logic*. 8th ed. London.

Mills, C. Wright. 1949. "The Contributions of Sociology to Industrial Relations." Pp. 199–222 in *Proceedings of the First Annual Meeting of the Industrial Relations Research Association*, edited by Milton Derber. Cleveland, Ohio: Industrial Relations Research Association.

Mills, Theodore M. and Frank E. Jones. 1965. "In Memoriam: Kaspar D. Naegele (1923–1965)." *American Sociological Review* 30: 579–81.

Montaigne, Michel de. 1947 [1580]. *Essays*. Translated by Charles Cotton. Garden City, NY: Doubleday.

Naegele, Kaspar D. 1948. "Jewish Contributions to Social Theory: A Suggestion for Further Research." Student Paper, Harvard University. Social Relations 113 (December). Naegele Papers.

Naegele, Kaspar D. 1949a. "Emotion and Family: Some General Considerations." Student Paper, Harvard University. Social Relations 132 (June). Naegele Papers.

Naegele, Kaspar D. 1949b. "From DeTocqueville to Myrdal: A Research Memorandum on Selected Studies of American Values." *Comparative Study of Values Working Papers*, No. 1 (October). Laboratory of Social Relations, Harvard University. Naegele Papers.

Naegele, Kaspar D. 1953. Letter to Oswald Hall, 9 April. Naegele Papers.

Naegele, Kaspar D. 1954. Letter to Talcott Parsons, 21 April. Parsons Papers, PP, CRP 1953–1955, Box 2.

Naegele, Kaspar D. 1956. "The Necessity of Bedevilment." *The Canadian Forum* 36 (November): 176–79.

Naegele, Kaspar D. 1957. "The Social Context of Communication." *Hospital Administration* 2: 32–43.

Naegele, Kaspar D. 1958. "Attachment and Alienation: Complementary Aspects of the Work of Durkheim and Simmel." *American Journal of Sociology* 63: 580–89.

Naegele, Kaspar D. 1961. "Some Observations on the Scope of Sociological Analysis." Pp. 3–29 in Parsons, et al. 1961.

Naegele, Kaspar D. 1970. *Health and Healing.* Compiled and edited by Elaine Cumming. San Francisco: Jossey-Bass.

Naegele, Philipp O. 1970. "Foreword." Pp. ix–xviii in Kaspar Naegele, *Health and Healing.*

Nelson, Benjamin N. 1969. *The Idea of Usury: From Tribal Brotherhood to Universal Otherhood*, 2nd ed., Enlarged. Chicago: University of Chicago Press.

Oakes, Guy. 1977. "Introduction: Simmel's Problematic." Pp. 1–37 in Georg Simmel, *The Problems of the Philosophy of History: An Epistemological Essay.* Translated and Edited by Guy Oakes. New York: The Free Press.

Oakes, Guy. 1980. "Introduction." Pp. 3–94 in Georg Simmel, *Essays on Interpretation in Social Science.* Translated and Edited by Guy Oakes. Totowa, NJ: Rowman and Littlefield.

Oromaner, Mark. 1980. "Erving Goffman and the Academic Community." *Philosophy of the Social Sciences* 10: 287–91.

Paharik, James G. 1983. "Park and Simmel: A Study in the Development of Systematic Sociological Theory." Unpublished Ph.D. dissertation. University of Pittsburgh.

Park, Robert E. n.d. Untitled autobiographical sketch, Robert E. Park Papers, Addenda, Box 1, University of Chicago.

Park, Robert E. 1915. "The City," *American Journal of Sociology* 20: 577–612.

Park, Robert E. 1923. Review of *The Negro in Chicago*, by the Chicago Commission on Race Relations, in *The New Republic* 34 (April 11): 194, 196.

Park, Robert E. 1926. "Behind Our Masks." *Survey Graphic* 56 (May): 135–139.

Park, Robert E. 1950 [1937]. "The Etiquette of Race Relations in the South." Pp. 177–88 in his *Race and Culture: Essays in the Sociology of Contemporary Man.* New York: Free Press.

Park, Robert E. and Ernest W. Burgess. 1969 [1921]. *Introduction to the Science of Sociology.* Chicago: University of Chicago Press.

Parsons, Edward S. 1912. *The Social Message of Jesus: A Course in Twelve Lessons.* New York: National Board of the YWCA.

Parsons, Talcott. nd. Manuscript of *Structure of Social Action.* PP, MSSA, Boxes 1–3.

Parsons, Talcott. 1929. "Sociology and Social Ethics: Proposed Outline of General Field." PP, MLNA 1929–1978, Box 1.

Parsons, Talcott. 1930. "Method and Technique of Sociological Research." PP, CM 1930s–1960s, Box 1.

Parsons, Talcott. 1932a. "Pareto and the Problems of Positivistic Sociology." PP, UM 1929–1967, Box 1.

Parsons, Talcott. 1932b. "[Review of] Ferdinand Toennies, *Einfuhrung in die Soziologie.*" PP, UM 1929–1967, Box 1.

Parsons, Talcott. 1934. "Some Reflections on 'The Nature and Significance of Economics.'" *Quarterly Journal of Economics* 48 (May): 511–45.

Parsons, Talcott. 1935a. "Prolegomena to a Theory of Institutions." PP, UM 1929–1967, Box 1.

Parsons, Talcott. 1935b. "The Place of Ultimate Values in Sociological Theory." *International Journal of Ethics* 45:282–316.

Parsons, Talcott. 1936 "*Georg Simmel* and *Ferdinand Toennies*: Social Relationships and the Elements of Action." PP, UM 1929–1967, Box 2.

Parsons, Talcott. 1951. *The Social System.* New York: The Free Press.

Parsons, Talcott. 1954. Letter to Kaspar Naegele, 24 March. PP, CRP 1953–1955, Box 2.

Parsons, Talcott. 1958. Letter to Kaspar Naegele, 5 September. PP, CRP 1930–1959, Box 15.

Parsons, Talcott. 1968 [1937]. *The Structure of Social Action*. New York: Free Press.

Parsons, Talcott. 1979. Letter to Jeffrey Alexander, 19 January. PP, CRP 1965–1979, Box 1.

Parsons, Talcott. 1981 [1978]. "Revisiting the Classics Throughout a Long Career." Pp. 183–194 in *The Future of the Sociological Classics*, edited by Buford Rhea. London: Allen & Unwin.

Parsons, Talcott, Edward Shils, Kaspar D. Naegele, and Jesse R. Pitts, eds. 1961. *Theories of Society*. New York: The Free Press.

Paulsen, Friedrich. 1906. *German Universities and University Study*. Translated by Frank Thilly and William W. Elwang. New York: Scribners.

Powell, Walter W. and Richard Robbins, eds. 1984. *Conflict and Consensus: A Festschrift in Honor of Lewis A. Coser*. New York: The Free Press.

Pugh, Anthony R. 1974. *Balzac's Recurring Characters*. Toronto: University of Toronto Press.

Raushenbush, Winifred. 1969. Letter to Donald N. Levine. 8 June, Robert E. Park Papers Addenda, Box 7, University of Chicago Library.

Raushenbush, Winifred. 1979. *Robert E. Park: Biography of a Sociologist*. Durham, NC: Duke University Press.

Riggins, Stephen Harold, ed. 1990. *Beyond Goffman: Studies on Communication, Institution, and Social Interaction*. New York: Mouton de Gruyter.

Robertson, J.M. 1909. Review of *Die Probleme der Geschichtsphilosophie: Eine Erkenntnistheoretische Studie*, 3rd ed., by Georg Simmel. *The Sociological Review* 2: 297–300.

Roethlisberger, F.J. 1941. *Management and Morale*. Cambridge: Harvard University Press.

Roethlisberger, F.J. and W.J. Dickson. 1939. *Management and the Worker*. Cambridge: Harvard University Press.

Rosenberg, Bernard. 1984. "An Interview with Lewis Coser," Pp. 17–52 in *Conflict and Consensus*, edited by Walter W. Powell and Richard Robbins. New York: Free Press.

Ross, Dorothy. 1991. *The Origins of American Social Science*. New York: Cambridge University Press.

Ross, Edward Alsworth. 1936. *Seventy Years of It: An Autobiography*. NY: D. Appleton-Century.

Roth, Guenther. 1992. "Interpreting and Translating Max Weber." *International Sociology* 7: 449–59.

Rule, James B. 1988. *Theories of Civil Violence*. Berkeley: University of California Press.

Salomon, Albert. 1943. "Simmel, Georg." Pp. 542–43 in *Universal Jewish Encyclopedia*, edited by Isaac Landman. New York: Universal Jewish Encyclopedia.

Salomon, Albert. 1945. "German Sociology." In *Twentieth Century Sociology*, edited by Georges Gurvitch and Wilbert Moore. New York: The Philosophical Library.

Salomon, Albert. 1955. *The Tyrrany of Progress: Reflections on the Origins of Sociology*. New York: Noonday Press.

Sandburg, Carl. 1969 [1919]. *The Chicago Race Riots: July, 1919*. New York: Harcourt, Brace & World.

Schrecker, Ellen W. 1986. *No Ivory Tower: McCarthyism and The Universities*. New York: Oxford University Press.

Schutz, Alfred. 1967. *The Phenomenology of the Social World*. Evanston, IL: Northwestern University Press.

Schutz, Alfred. 1971 [1944]. "The Stranger." Pp. 91–105 in *Collected Papers, Vol. II. Studies in Social Theory*. The Hague: Martinus Nijhoff.

Seidman, Steven. 1992. "Theory as Narrative with Moral Intent." Pp. 47–81 in *Postmodernism and Social Theory*, edited by Steven Seidman and David Wagner. Oxford: Basil Blackwell.

Sewny, Vahan D. 1967. *The Social Theory of James Mark Baldwin*. NY: Augustus M. Kelley.

Sheppard, Harold. 1948. "Managerial Sociology." Ph.D. diss. University of Wisconsin, Madison.

Sheppard, Harold. 1949. "The Treatment of Unionism in 'Managerial Sociology.'" *American Sociological Review* 14: 310–13.

Shibutani, Tamotsu. 1962. "Reference Groups and Social Control." In *Human Behavior and Social Process*, edited by Arnold M. Rose. Boston: Houghton Mifflin.

Shils, Edward and Talcott Parsons. n.d. "[List of selections for] *The Sources of Sociological Theory: A Reader*." PP, MBMW, Box 6.

Simmel, Arnold. 1981. Letter to the author, 13 May.

Simmel, Georg. 1890. *Über sociale Differenzierung*. Leipzig: Dunker & Humblot.

Simmel, Georg. 1895. "L' influence du nombre des unités sociales sur les charactères des sociétés," *Annales de l'Institut International de Sociologie*. 1. Paris: Giard & E. Brière.

Simmel, Georg. 1896. "Superiority and Subordination as Subject-Matter of Sociology, I and II." *American Journal of Sociology* 2: 167–89; 392–415.

Simmel, Georg. 1902. "Tendencies in German Life and Thought Since 1870." *International Monthly* 5: 166–84.

Simmel, Georg. 1904. "Fashion." *International Quarterly* 10: 130–55.

Simmel, Georg. 1922. *Lebensanschauung: vier metaphysische Kapitel*, 2nd ed. Munich & Leipzig: Duncker & Humblot.

Simmel, Georg. 1949. "The Sociology of Sociability." Translated by Everett C. Hughes. *American Journal of Sociology* 7: 254–61.

Simmel, Georg. 1950. *The Sociology of Georg Simmel*. Translated, edited, and with an introduction by Kurt H. Wolff. New York: Free Press.

Simmel Georg. 1955. *Conflict and The Web of Group Affiliations*. Translated by Kurt H. Wolff and Reinhard Bendix. New York: Free Press.

Simmel, Georg. 1959. *Sociology of Religion*. Translated by Curt Rosenthal. New York: Philosophical Library.

Simmel, Georg. 1968. *The Conflict in Modern Culture and Other Essays*. Translated and with an Introduction by K. Peter Etzkorn. New York: Teachers College Press.

Simmel, Georg. 1976a [1918]. "The Conflict of Modern Culture," Pp. 223–42 in Peter Lawrence, *Georg Simmel: Sociologist and European*. New York: Barnes & Noble.

Simmel, Georg. 1976b [1917]. "The Crisis of Culture," Pp. 223–42 in Peter Lawrence, *Georg Simmel: Sociologist and European*. New York: Barnes & Noble.

Simmel, Georg. 1980 [1918]. "On the Nature of Historical Understanding." Pp. 97–126 in *Georg Simmel: Essays on Interpretation in Social Science*. Translated, edited, and with an introduction by Guy Oakes. Totowa, NJ: Rowman and Littlefield.

Simmel, Georg, et. al. 1965. *Essays on Philosophy and Aesthetics*. Edited by Kurt H. Wolff. New York: Harper & Row.

Simpson, Ida Harper. 1972. "Continuities in the Sociology of Everett C. Hughes." *Sociological Quarterly* 13: 547–58.

Small, Albion. 1895a. "The Era of Sociology." *American Journal of Sociology* 1: 1–15.

Small, Albion. 1895b. Review of *Annales de l'Institut International de Sociologie. Travaux de premier Congrès tenu à Paris. American Journal of Sociology* 1: 218–19.

Small, Albion. 1896a. Review of Arthur Fairbanks, *An Introduction to Sociology. American Journal of Sociology* 2: 305–10.

Small, Albion. 1896b. Review of A. Schäffle, *Bau und Leben des socialen Körpers. American Journal of Sociology* 2: 310–15.

Small, Albion. 1896c. "Scholarship and Social Agitation." *American Journal of Sociology* 1: 564–82.

Small, Albion. 1898. "The Methodology of the Social Problem." *American Journal of Sociology* 4: 380–94.

Small, Albion. 1899. "The Value of Sociology to Working Pastors." *The Outlook* 62 (June 17): 389–92.

Small, Albion. 1902. Review of Franklin Henry Giddings, *Inductive Sociology. American Journal of Sociology* 7: 557–58.

Small, Albion. 1905a. *General Sociology: An Exposition of the Main Development in Sociological Theory from Spencer to Ratzenhofer.* Chicago: University of Chicago Press.

Small, Albion. 1905b. "Research Ideals." *The University of Chicago Record* 10: 87.

Small, Albion. 1909. Review of *Soziologie,* by Georg Simmel. *American Journal of Sociology* 14: 544–45.

Small, Albion. 1916. "Fifty Years of Sociology in the United States (1865–1915)." *American Journal of Sociology* 21: 177–269.

Small, Albion. 1925. Review of Nicholas Spykman, *The Social Theory of Georg Simmel. American Journal of Sociology* 31: 84–87.

Smith, Gregory. 1989. "A Simmelian Reading of Goffman." Unpublished Ph.D. Dissertation, University of Salford.

Smith, Gregory. 1994 [1989]. "Snapshots 'Sub Specie Aeternitatis': Simmel, Goffman and Formal Sociology." Pp. 354–83 in *Georg Simmel: Critical Assessments,* Vol. 3, edited by David Frisby. London: Routledge.

Smith, Gregory, ed. 1996. *Goffman's Patrimony: Studies in a Sociological Legacy.* London: Routledge.

Sorensen, Robert C. 1951. "The Concept of Conflict in Industrial Sociology." *Social Forces* 29: 263–67.

154   REFERENCES

Sorokin, Pitirim A. 1965. *Fads and Foibles in Modern Sociology*. Chicago: Regnery.

Spencer, Herbert. 1969 [1882]. *Principles of Sociology*. Abridged Edition. Hamden, CT: Archon Books.

Spykman, Nicholas J. 1926. "A Social Philosophy of the City." *American Journal of Sociology* 20: 47–55.

Spykman, Nicholas J. 1942. *America's Strategy in World Politics: The United States and the Balance of Power*. New York: Harcourt, Brace.

Spykman, Nicholas J. 1966 [1925]. *The Social Theory of Georg Simmel*. New York: Atherton Press.

Stauth, Georg and Bryan S. Turner. 1988. *Nietzsche's Dance: Resentment, Reciprocity and Resistance in Social Life*. New York: Basil Blackwell.

Stehr, Nico. 1986. "Sociological Theory and Practical Reason: The Restriction of the Scope of Sociological Theory." Pp. 36–43 in *Sociological Theory in Transition*, edited by Mark L. Wardell and Stephen P. Turner. Boston: Allen & Unwin.

Storr, Richard J. 1953. *The Beginnings of Graduate Education in America*. Chicago: University of Chicago Press.

Strong, P.M. 1988. "Minor Courtesies and Macro Structures." Pp. 228–49 in *Erving Goffman: Exploring the Interation Order*, edited by Paul Drew and Anthony Wootton. Boston: Northeastern University Press.

Sztompka, Piotr. 1986. *Robert K. Merton: An Intellectual Profile*. New York: St. Martin's Press.

Thon, O. 1897. "The Present Status of Sociology in Germany, I, II, III." *American Journal of Sociology* 2: 567–88; 718–36; 792–800.

Travers, Andrew. 1996. "Non-Person and Goffman: Sociology Under the Influence of Literature." In *Goffman's Patrimony*, edited by Greg Smith. London: Routledge.

Tufts, James H. 1896. "Recent Sociological Tendencies in France." *American Journal of Sociology* 1: 446–56.

Turner, Ralph H. 1962. "Role Taking: Process versus Conformity," in *Human Behavior and Social Process*, edited by Arnold M. Rose. New York: Houghton Mifflin.

Turner, Ralph H. 1967. "Introduction" to *Robert E. Park: On Social Control and Collective Behavior*. Chicago: University of Chicago Press.

Turner, Stephen Park and Jonathan H. Turner. 1992. *The Impossible Science: An Institutional Analysis of American Sociology*. Newbury Park, CA: Sage.

Verhoeven, Jeff. 1993. "An Interview with Erving Goffman, 1980." *Research on Language and Social Interaction* 26/3: 317–48.

Vidich, Arthur J. 1991. "Baudrillard's *America*: Lost in the Ultimate Simulacrum," *Theory, Culture & Society* 8: 135–44.

Vidich, Arthur J. and Stanford M. Lyman. 1985. *American Sociology: Worldly Rejections of Religion and Their Directions*. New Haven: Yale University Press.

Vidich, Arthur J. and Stanford M. Lyman. 1986. "State, Ethics and Public Morality in American Sociological Thought." Pp. 44–56 in *Sociological Theory in Transition*, edited by Mark L. Wardell and Stephen R. Turner. Boston: Allen & Unwin.

Vincent, George. 1896. "The Province of Sociology." *American Journal of Sociology* 1: 473–91.

Wagner, Helmut R. ed. 1970. *Alfred Schutz: On Phenomenology and Social Relations*. Chicago: University of Chicago Press.

Wald, Alan M. 1987. *The New York Intellectuals: The Rise and Decline of the Anti-Stalinist Left from the 1930's to the 1980's*. Chapel Hill: University of North Carolina Press.

Weingartner, Rudolph H. 1962. *Experience and Culture: The Philosophy of Georg Simmel*. Middletown, CT: Wesleyan University Press.

Weinstein, Deena and Michael A. Weinstein. 1989. "Simmel and the Dialectic of the Double Boundary." *Sociological Inquiry* 59: 38–49.

Weinstein, Deena and Michael A. Weinstein. 1990a. "Dimensions of Conflict: Georg Simmel on Modern Life." Pp. 341–55 in *Georg Simmel and Contemporary Sociology*, edited by Michael Kaern, et al. Boston: Kluwer.

Weinstein, Deena and Michael A. Weinstein. 1990b. "Simmel and the Theory of Postmodern Society." Pp. 75–87 in *Theories of Modernity and Postmodernity*, edited by Bryan S. Turner. Newbury Park, CA: Sage.

Weinstein Deena and Michael A. Weinstein. 1991. "Georg Simmel: Sociological ~~Flaneur~~ Bricoleur." *Theory, Culture & Society* 8: 151–68.

Weinstein, Deena and Michael A. Weinstein. 1993. *Postmodern(ized) Simmel*. New York: Routledge.

Whitehead, T. North. 1938. *The Industrial Worker*. Cambridge: Harvard University Press.

Winkin, Yves. 1984. "Entretien avec Erving Goffman." *Actes de la recherche en sciences sociales* 54 (September): 85–87. Reprinted in Winkin 1988.

Winkin Yves. 1988. "Erving Goffman: Portrait de sociologue en juene homme." Pp. 13–92 in *Erving Goffman: Les Moments et Leurs Hommes*, edited and introduced by Yves Winkin. Paris: Seuil.

Winkin, Yves. 1996. "Erving Goffman: What Is a Life? The Uneasy Making of an Intellectual Biography." In *Goffman's Patrimony*, edited by Greg Smith. London: Routledge.

Wolff, Kurt H. 1950. "Introduction." In *The Sociology of Georg Simmel*, translated and edited by Kurt H. Wolff. New York: Free Press.

Wolff, Kurt H., ed. 1959. *Georg Simmel: 1858–1918: A Collection of Essays with Translations and a Bibliography*. Columbus: The Ohio State University Press.

Wolff, Kurt H. 1977. Review of *Ästhetik und Soziologie um die Jahrhundertwende: Georg Simmel*, edited by Hannes Böhringer and Karlfried Gründer. *American Journal of Sociology* 83: 224–27.

INDEX

Abel, Theodore, 50
Adams, Henry, 10
Aggasiz, Louis, 6
Alexander, Jeffrey, 55, 58
American exceptionalism, xi
American Journal of Sociology, 7, 9
    table 1, 13, 64, 76–77, 126
American prospect: Simmel and,
    xi–xii
anarchism: Simmel's critique of,
    13
"anticipation," 117
Anti-semitism: in England, 98; in
    France, 98; in Germany, 97–98,
    107; and Simmel, 95–98
Arendt, Hannah, 128
Augustine, Saint, 110

Baeck, Leo (Institute), xvi, 92
Bakewell, Charles M., 8, 125
Baldwin, James Mark, 18–19, 32
Balzac, Honoré de, 91, 134
Baudrillard, Jean, 119
Becker, Howard P., 59, 130
Bell, Daniel, 66
Bendix, Reinhard, 22, 65–66
Berger, Peter, ix
Bergson, Henri, 94
Besnard, Philippe, 75
Bierstedt, Robert, 72–73
Blau, Peter, 70–71
Blumer, Herbert, 82

Bouglé, Célestin, 80
British Museum, 126
Broyles Commission, 25
Burgess, Ernest W., 25, 31, 127

Comte, August, 11, 47
Cooley, Charles H., 46, 76
Coser, Lewis A.: biography of,
    79–81; dissertation of, 69, 81;
    "double career"of, 87; and
    Freud, 85; on industrial
    relations, 81–83; and Marxism,
    79–81, 83, 86; and Merton, 81,
    83; on realistic and
    nonrealistic conflict, 86;
    safety-valve theory of conflict,
    39, 84–86; on Simmel as
    "stranger in the academy,"
    113–115

Darwin, Charles, 10
Dilthey, Wilhelm, 5, 94, 96
Doyle, Bertram W.: and E. C.
    Hughes, 129; and Herbert
    Spencer, 33–35; on "playing at"
    etiquette, 35
Duncan, Hugh Dalziel, 22
Durkheim, Emile, 30, 46, 47, 50,
    52, 98, 89, 91, 98, 126; and
    Simmel compared, 64–65,
    75–76